DYING TO LIVE

LEARN TO LIVE A FULL LIFE FROM YOUR LIVED EXPERIENCES

Christine Dernederlanden C.B.T., C.T.S.S.

Robert's Press Empowering People Through Life's Challenges
www.robertspress.ca
Ph: 905-688-8009
Toll Free: 1-866-582-5558
To learn more about the author
www.christinedernederlanden.ca

Author Christine Dernederlanden C.B.T., C.T.S.S.
Humanitarian in the field of Grief & Trauma
Edited by Laura E. Pasquale, Ph.D.
Cover & Layout Design: Ashley Santoro
Copyright © 2020 Robert's Press
No part of this book may be reproduced or copied in any form without written permission from the publisher, Robert's Press
ISBN: 978-0-9686762-8-8

Disclaimer

This is a work of non-fiction. Nonetheless, the stories are derived from numerous experiences combined to create a story that depicts a lesson or to display a certain behaviour. Any resulting resemblance to persons living or dead is entirely coincidental and unintentional. This publication is not intended as a substitute for the advice of health care professionals.

Dedicated to my family
for their support in a career that chose me.
I could have never done this on my own.
Thank you Nathan, Jacob, Chelsea and Coralea

Follow a humanitarian's twenty-year journey beyond 9/11. It takes courage to confront life and death, health and recovery.

Please consider your own readiness as you work through the suggested activities in this book.

This book includes purposeful pages for mindfulness and meditation colouring.

TABLE OF CONTENTS

Acknowledgement	6
Preface	7
Chapter One: Learning Through Lived Experience	8
Chapter Two: The Bottle of Burdens	16
Chapter Three: Perception	28
Chapter Four: The Science of Emotions	40
Pinwheel of Emotions	47
Chapter Five: The Body's Expression	49
Our Love is Inseparable	51
Chapter Six: What Masks Do You Wear?	55
Chapter Seven: The Gift of "the Seeing"	66
Chapter Eight: Are We Creating Our Own Reflections?	73
The Mirror of your Memories	77
Chapter Nine: Cutting the Cord	82
Cutting the Cord of Connection	84
Forgiving Flowers	88
Chapter Ten: Why Do We Feel Pain?	93
Chapter Eleven: Continuing to Live	101
Chapter Twelve: The Perspective That Matters is Your Own!	107
Chapter Thirteen: How Fitting	112
About the Author	118

ACKNOWLEDGEMENT

I would be remiss if I did not mention the day I completed my last word on these pages. The world was hit with a pandemic. Covid-19 swarmed across countries worldwide. I was called to aid the children and the youth during this time. Working side by side with our youth, I created *Cora and the Corona One Little Girl's Journey to Healing in Quarantine*. The story aided more than 7,500 mental health essential workers, schools, hospitals and so many more.

To evolve with the changes in the world as we strive to return to a full life, *Cora and the Corona Course: Helping Children Understand Invisible Viruses* was developed. The course was designed to help implement virus safety measures in schools, and in programs or organizations that serve children and youth. The goal of the course is to empower our youth with the confidence to practice virus safety measures and to support each other during this time. The course touches on safety precautions, emotional and mental wellbeing, communication, recycling and friendship... with an ultimate end goal of making our world a better place for all!

And to that end, I wish you fuller living and happy reading.

PREFACE

This book is about learning through lived experiences. You will take a journey with me as I share my lived experience. You will laugh, cry and relate, as we all strive to live a full life. Each chapter shares stories of life events that I experienced and the lessons I learned along the way.

But this book is not just about me; it is about YOU! Yes, you will learn through your lived experiences as well, as each chapter gives you an activity to perform. The book will teach you to document your life by writing your lived experiences down or by sharing the lessons you have learned with others.

Learning through lived experiences can be addictive. Your perspective on new situations becomes broadened, and you see things in many different lights, understanding there is no one way to look at things. It is exciting to explore your mind, emotions, past, body, all of it! As you'll learn through the experience of reading and engaging in this book, we are all *Dying to Live a Full Life!*

CHAPTER ONE:
LEARNING THROUGH LIVED EXPERIENCE

During my younger years in school I was placed in the S.L.D. class, which stood for the "Special Learning Disability" class. My friends coined us the "Stupid Little Dummies" class instead. Thinking of this triggers my PTSD, as I am reminded of the horrors of grade school. Here I learned that, if you didn't fit the norm or into the standard box ideal of what a student should be, you were considered to have a learning disability. Well, I was the round peg, and my teachers couldn't quite figure out how I was gaining the box knowledge in a circular way. Meaning that I was understanding the course work, but in a different way from the norm. In turn they gave me a comprehension disability label and decided to integrate me into the odd normal kids class, for a lack of better words.

That was in the 1980's (perhaps you remember this decade). I was tested regularly as to how I was learning, and when high school came along, I was earmarked for a vocational school. I was not planning to attend this school at all. I asked to be allowed to attend Dennis Morris High School, a regular academic school. I clearly realized I was different from most students but never thought I was behind them. Once my parents pushed back against the school, along with some help from school support, they agreed I could attend the high school of my choice, but in all basic classes.

Then, during the summer just before my grade school prom, my brother suddenly fell over the Niagara Falls Gorge to his death. This accident devastated my family and community. I share more about this tragedy within these pages, but this event truly affected my academic learning. I saw things quite differently now. I became very interested in and was impacted by others' emotions, actions, and behaviours as well as why people respond so differently to trauma. I started to play with my appearance, language and actions to evoke reactions from people. Not only was I a six-foot redhead, I was the girl who was rumored to have a brother who jumped over Niagara Falls (so untrue... I will share more later on).

Then I donned a set of crutches, having had a cancer scare that literally taught me that internalizing your emotions is not a good idea, and that emotions always find a way to express themselves, even physically through our bodies. This was a lot to comprehend at fourteen, especially for someone who had been diagnosed as having a comprehension problem.

My high school years were filled with people either talking to me slowly, as if I couldn't understand them, or people walking the other way as I scared them with my rather large presence. I actually felt, later on in high school, that I was accepted and understood quite well. But that didn't happen all in one day. My class size consisted of a closet of three people and a teacher, who frequently changed.

I recall sitting next to this young guy who was on the

football team named Trevor. He was quite good looking with broad shoulders. One day I turned to him and questioned, "Why are you in the closet taking basic courses?" He replied, "I don't seem to pass English," as he pushed his paper over to me. The title on his page read, "What I dream." I giggled and replied, "To be healthy, have no sorrow, no sadness, no death." To this he replied, "Impossible dream." I lowered my head and my eyes filled (as they do now as I type). I replied, "Maybe not," thinking to myself, *What if we learned about it, understood it more, death, trauma?*

He laughed and then said, "You're weird."

We both started to giggle as I said, "I guess that's a little heavy...?"

Together we talked about what he dreamed of. As he spoke I motioned for him to write it down. I sat listening as he explained in detail the famous, fastest, best looking football player of all time. Our closet was more than a closet that day.

I plugged along with my crutches to each class as the school attempted to integrate me into the so-called normal stream of teenagers. I would balance my crutches as I kicked the doors open to pass through the halls. Quickly I learned the value of being sick and how to use it. Often I would ask a friend to carry my bag so we could get out of class early to beat the rush in the halls. I became popular over that one.

One day a teacher asked me to stay behind. As everyone left the classroom I saw his tall frame sway back and forth as he cleaned the chalkboard. He started to talk softly, as if he was going to tell me something bad. I knew my marks didn't reflect how well I thought I was doing. This seemed to be a common thing (I would think that I wrote the correct answers and would leave the exam feeling like I had aced it, to only find out I had failed), so I exhaled and waited for the bad news.

He came over to me and placed a test on the desk and said, "If I mark this backwards, you pass."

I sat confused. "What???"

He walked up to the clean chalk board and said, "What do you see?" As he started to write numbers, I read them out loud. Then he said, "Read them from this side," pointing to the other end of the numbers. "

That's backwards!!" I exclaimed, to which he responded, "Try it," so I did.

I took the numbers into my mind and spun them in every direction possible, until I was able to read them backwards out loud to the teacher. It fascinated me how the numbers had so many angles and variations in my mind.

He then said, "Follow me. What if this is the way to read numbers?"

I replied in a loud voice, "Everyone is backwards?"

He laughed out loud with a huge belly laugh, "No, what if you are backwards". The light bulb shone bright as my mind spun with thoughts. *All I have to do is flip everything for others to understand me. Is it really that easy? How is this possible?*

The next day I started secretly reading things from the other end. I learned quickly that what my mind could do with numbers and letters, my hands could also do. I saw that at times I didn't pick up the pen with the same hand every day. I started to see now that, when I wrote essays, the end of the story sounded as good as the beginning. I started to flip everything I did, even if this looked extremely wrong to me. I was so scared that a teacher would exclaim, "What is this…..?"as I handed in my first essay.

When everyone left the class the next week, I heard my name called to stay after class. This teacher was very gentle, as you can imagine any religion teacher being. She placed the essay on the desk in front of me, and I gulped as I glared directly at the large red "A" in front of me. She then said, "This is excellent, you really were able to share your perspective. Whatever you're doing, keep it up." I hopped out of the class on my crutches with a spring in my foot just like Tigger from *Winnie The Pooh*. Life changed as I started to get it! *People were backwards!*

As the years passed in high school, my leg healed, and I struggled with learning to trust my leg and walk again. On top of that, I missed Robert a lot. I found a not-so-healthy-but-healthier-than-most way to balance being a teenager and all this stuff I was dealing with in my personal life. I called this coping method "The Bottle of Burdens", which I will explain in depth in the chapters to come. Using this method and my newfound learning style, I was able to integrate into the so-called normal classes, and no one knew how or why I was able to now. I kept my secret to myself and thanked that teacher every day!

I graduated from high school with a scholarship for Family Studies, which was unreal to me! On top of that, I was the only student to ever achieve all A's in the study of family dynamics and societal behaviours. In 2017, I had the honour of being a recipient of the Dennis Morris High School

Distinguished Alumni of The Year! As I spoke at the graduation that year to an auditorium of young hopeful graduates, they stood to applaud me, because I highlighted how "normal" is different for everyone. Normal is your authentic self, shining through.

Later in life I was given the opportunity to return to college or a university. Niagara University in the U.S. offered me a scholarship to study social work. But before I started school, they asked me to get an educational assessment by numerous professionals in the field. Because this came after my deployment and aiding to Ground Zero after the 9/11 attacks, I thought it best to go forward with the testing, both educationally and emotionally. But I was a little set back when they interviewed my husband.

He openly said, "Just flip everything she says or does, then it makes sense. For directions, always go left if she says right." Then he followed it up with, "It usually only happens when she is tired." (For sure, it does!)

Do you know how hard it is to flip everything every moment of the day? I figured the guy I married should just flip everything my way.

As the test started, I thought it silly. I played with cubes and pictures, answered questions, and read stories for days and days. Then, I sat with another person who wanted to talk about my emotions. I started to share stories from my life, but he stopped me and said, "Share about your emotions, not the story of your life". I then began to cry, and cry and cry, for days.

After numerous days of release and acceptance of

who I truly am, the results were finally in! I sat as they placed graphs and charts with coloured lines in front of me. They explained how I could be ambidextrous, meaning that I use both hands. They then told me I had a form of dyslexia, but have learned to compensate for it immensely. One thing they did comment on was their amazement at my oral communication skills. They pulled a graph out that showed the standard score for the area of oral communication and then revealed my score... which extended beyond the page. They informed me that I was superior, beyond the average person, in oral communication, which encompassed reading emotions, body language, the ability to connect with others, and to evaluate a situation and react accordingly. Essentially, I had perfected communication with people in all its forms. They were fascinated that I found a way to understand people beyond their verbal capacities. Since I could not understand the written word or the spoken word, that is, the meaning of words, I found a way to read people based on all other bodily senses.

    At the end of my first year at Niagara University I had achieved all A's in my classes, this time with no special learning disability label. I was offered the opportunity to develop and work in camps commissioned by the United Nations Friendship Ambassadors and the Lions International. This led me to the decision of putting my superior talents to work and leaving school for those camps.

    I wanted to share this story about my journey of educational learning, because it plays a huge role in how I see the world and the perspective I take, a perspective which was ultimately different right from birth. During my years in aiding, I clearly learned that, emotionally, we all learn differently too. No two people process a tragedy the same way. There are fundamental differences. Small, but still there, these differences can have an impact on the healing process. Also, how we perceive things and how we respond to them differs greatly. That is where being superior in my area of expertise works well. I never approach a topic the same way with different people, because what people have experienced in life and how they handled it creates who they are.

So putting that into perspective, we are experiential learners in the area of emotional sorrow, sadness, death and grief. Educationally, we can be told how to react sensibly to traumatic situations, but no educational institution can predict or tell you how you as an individual will act in a traumatic situation. Only your past can give you that insight. What you have learned before, through lived experiences, will filter up and will either aid or disable you through the next lived experience. Essentially, if you loved someone and that ended in divorce, the mind, emotions and body will all say, "We lived this experience before and it didn't end well. Move cautiously." But not all lived experiences are bad, some are great, and we relive them… a lot.

CHAPTER TWO:
THE BOTTLE OF BURDENS

I once worked with a woman who was badly beaten after the death of her mother. She felt enormous guilt for her mother's death and felt she deserved to be beaten. I sat and listened to her irrational thoughts about her situation, knowing if I corrected her it would not be heard. I know that a person has to come to her own realizations in order to make real change. As she sobbed, tears rolled down her cheeks all the way to the crevices along her neck.

I handed her a tissue as she looked up with big puffy eyes surrounded by blue bruises. She took the tissue and said, "My pain is nothing compared to what you have seen. You have aided in world tragedies".

I took her hand in mine and replied, "No, yours is worse; you think you're alone in your pain. During world tragedies people unite, they help in many ways. You, my friend, think you're alone… that is scary." She smiled as she began to realize that she was not alone in her grief.

We don't share our pain willingly with others, but we need to, in order to heal and move on. Sadly, too many times in today's society we try to save face, and keep up with people who don't really exist. We try to have this amazing Facebook profile to showcase our amazing lives, but that is often not the truth. I am here to tell you, you're not alone in your pain, and no one really believes your Facebook profile either.

We all carry burdens. Some call them ghosts in the closet, or their dirty laundry. There are numerous names for what we keep inside and don't share with others. I once gave a presentation, and a woman stood to ask a question. She was older, wearing a blue floral blouse and was well put together. She had a beautiful English accent. She began to question me, "Why do we need to bring up the past and talk about it? It's over with; we are fine."

I replied, "Are we fine?"

She shot back, "Yes. I am happy".

For me, the only appropriate response to this was, "Then why are you at my workshop?"

She replied agitatedly, "To figure out why I dream of my past all the time". The room turned to look at her, and she smiled.

She had no idea of the connection her reactive subconscious mind had with her wise conscious mind. (The reactive unconscious mind is an immediate response without thought process to a situation or traumatic event. The wise conscious mind is a well thought out process before responding to an event.) She felt that because she didn't think of her past actively throughout the day, it couldn't be bothering her throughout the night. Perception is huge, and self-awareness comes with connecting to our authentic selves.

Just as this workshop participant could not connect the reactive unconscious mind to the wise conscious mind, some of us can't connect to the fact that we even have burdens. So the reactive unconscious mind will shuffle things down from the wise conscious mind, so they are not comprehended at times, to protect us. I often felt that the emotional denial that my reactive unconscious mind created had protected me from the reality of my life.

But as we age, the reactive unconscious mind overflows. That overflow is denied. The activity to follow covers the denial that I call "the bottle of burdens", and is practiced in order to bring forth some of your dark secrets within your reactive unconscious mind. I will admit that burdens or scary, traumatic events from the past are hard to even consider bringing forth in your mind on any level. Sometimes even happy burdens are good to review as well, if they have impacted your life greatly.

I would like to take a moment to define what burdens, grief and death mean. We often look at death as a loved one dying. But the grief that results from death is felt in all forms. We need to realize that a loss of any kind that results in human sorrow is grieved in a way similar to a death, but on a different emotional level. So essentially the death or loss of a home, relationship, employment, etc. are things that cause us to grieve and to feel human sorrow. Burdens are things that rise up often to bother you. Think of the reactive mind trying to shuffle them down from your wise conscious mind, such as when you try to move forward in life, but seem to not move, and your mind says, "You can't do that, because you always fail."

Before we start to really see how these burdens in our bottles affect us in our daily lives, let's look at our support systems. This will help to ground us as we do our work. What's a support system, you may ask? The people in your life that you connect with and share these burdens with. If there is no one, then that is perhaps our first place to start.

To define your support system, ponder these questions:

1. When something happy happens who do you first call to share it with? Why?

_____

_____

_____

2. When something bad or sad happens who do you first call to share it with? Why?

_____
_____
_____

3. With whom do you laugh the most? This includes animals.

_____
_____
_____

4. Who drains your energy? Who fills you with energy?

_____
_____
_____

5. Who do you love? Now who do you really love, without borders, without necessity?

_____
_____
_____

Now let's take a moment to put your support system into a heart support visual. Think of three hearts within each other. Place yourself in the centre of the smallest heart. Then, in the medium heart place, the names of people who are your support system. (Hint, they may be the people you named in your answers to the above questions).

Next, let's look at what's in your bottle of burdens. Here are some questions to ask yourself to help with this process:

1. Who has died in your life? Include any animals you were close to or any pets.

_____
_____

2. What other losses have you encountered? (Include divorce, friends just leaving the friendship, loss of a job, retirement, loss of limbs, loss of self-esteem, loss of connection with the world.)

_____
_____

3. Are you a caregiver for someone?

_____
_____

4. Did you experience trauma as a child? Loss of childhood?

_____
_____

5. What burdens, traumatic events and/or memories do you carry from your past? For myself an example would be special learning disability and aiding during the Sept. 11th terrorists attacks.

_____
_____

List all your burdens from most impactful to least impactful. Determine the impact level by your emotional and physical reaction to the recollection of the burden memory.

Ask yourself, after reviewing your list, how you feel about your bottle of burdens? Did you know it even existed? How do you think you might manage the bottle of burdens? The bottle of burdens is a visual image of your reactive unconscious mind shuffling down your deep secrets, past experiences and thoughts.

Now let's take a moment to go back to your heart support visual. The three hearts within each other, where you are the centre heart and your support system surrounds you. Now that we acknowledge that we could have or do have a bottle of burdens, let's address them. Let's dump it out! TOGETHER! Place your five core burdens in the outer heart.

These activities might sound crazy, I know! But I also know from personal experience how to manage a bottle of burdens quite well. As a teenager, after the death of my brother and a cancer scare, I started my own bottle. I filled it with everything I could think of, from being bullied to being in the Special Learning Disability Class, to feeling lonely at times. I found that I would just let the negative comments from others roll off my shoulders, smiling and trying to be happy all the time. When I got home, figuratively, I would take the top off the bottle, blare music and scream at the top of my lungs. No one could hear me as the music was way too loud or, if I was lucky, no one was home. It got a little harder when I went to college as my roommate never went out much. They would say, "What are you doing up there in your bedroom? Sounds like a herd of elephants."

We all have a bottle of burdens, and we all have to open them at times. For me it was screaming and dancing that relieved my burdens. I loved my bottle; it became a way of life that worked very well. Or so I thought.

How do you feel about your bottle of burdens now that you know it exists? Is it controlled and safe, or out of control; are you afraid to open it up, scared? How do you manage your bottle (overeat, scream it out, watch TV a lot, engage in excessive sports, exercise, drink, gamble, smoke, drugs, sex, get depressed, for example)?

Here is the biggest question: What if the bottle breaks? What happens?

During my time in Alberta speaking at Remembrance Ceremonies (which commemorated participants and loved ones who had died), I shared the bottle of burden analogy during my speech. When speaking, I always choke up when remembering how my parents sat in front of me, as the doctor told them their daughter might have bone cancer. I recall sitting just behind them as they kept it together, and I felt my stomach fall, thinking, *Wow, I may die?*

My own mortality came thrusting into my mind. What if I get to see Robert before anyone else? Part of me thought that might be okay, because I missed my brother so much. This is part of the reason that I find it so interesting when people only pair the word "grief" with death. I am here to tell you that there is much more pain out there, human sorrow of all kinds!

After sharing my story I invite others to spend time afterwards and share food and drinks as they share their stories too. One person caught me just as I was leaving for the night. They said, "Do you want to know when my bottle broke? I have no idea why it broke then." They explained that their cousin was physically disabled and couldn't walk. The father had asked them to bring their cousin in from the outside, and being a teenager, they forgot. Then someone proceeded to back up a tractor, having no idea the young cousin was still outside. That young child died. They continued. "I never thought about this until one day at confession. Why do you think it all came forward and I broke completely in confession?"

I directed the question back to them. But they could not see clearly; I don't think they wanted too. They didn't want to accept the reality of the situation at all. What I found so interesting was they could have had, for a moment, the glimpse of the realization that they may have unknowingly played a part in the death of that child? Or did they just decide to climb back in the bottle of burdens and not heal? I will let you decide your reasoning on this one.

Now when you think about it, most of us, when asked about our past burdens will not introduce them in this manner, "Hi, my name is Christine, and I have this amazing support system that has helped me through life challenges." We usually say, "Hi, I am Christine, and I lost my brother at the age of fourteen". We put our burden before our support system. But, what if, as in this chapter, we changed that? If we put our support system *before* our burdens as we did in this chapter? What if we realized we are not alone in our bottle of burdens? Perception is huge, as we'll see.

Before reading further, please know that there are many activities in the following chapters. You can put the book down and come back to them when you're ready, or pause at any time. Take your time with each activity. Don't rush them.

CHAPTER THREE: PERCEPTION

The hardest thing I have seen any individual struggle with is understanding and expressing their own emotions. We tend to either not express at all or to express way too much. Often, we do not truly focus on ourselves and the emotions we are expressing, but rather more on the person receiving the expression of our feelings.

Let's take a minute to play with all the norms that are considered to be acceptable or are coined within society. For example, women are considered over emotional and express too much. Men are strong and get angry fast. Both are stern type casts of genders. But in this work, there is no stern type cast of anyone. Let's discover how much of an emotion-based person you are. Neither end of the spectrum is good or bad, but rather just who you are. And who you are can come from a variety of factors.

Let's ponder a few questions. What came first, the egg or the chicken? I don't think anyone knows the answer to that. But when you think of yourself, what came first, your outer being, your body (shell), or your essence, mind or consciousness (the yoke that creates the chicken)? What causes us to see things the way we do? What causes us to react the way we react? Is it different for everyone? These are super-heavy, confusing questions that we all ponder at one point in our lives. Let's approach those questions from a different perspective. Take a moment to look at the picture below and answer a few questions.

1. What do you see?
   _____
   _____
   _____

2. How does it make you feel?
   _____
   _____
   _____

3. Why does it make you feel that way? Take your time and don't rush.
   _____
   _____
   _____

4. If I were to title the picture *Freedom,* how would it make you feel? Why do you feel that way after I titled it?
   _____
   _____
   _____

5. What would you name the picture? Why would you name it that?
   _____
   _____
   _____

Now take a moment and ponder what made you answer the questions above the way you did.

1. When I gave the picture a title, did your perception change? Meaning, did you see the picture as something different? Like a light bulb went off: *Oh, yeah, that makes sense now.* **Why did it make sense all of a sudden? Or why did it not change your perception?**

_____
_____
_____
_____
_____
_____

2. Can you relate this picture to your life? Share how it relates to your life and why you saw what you saw? Think: do you stand firm in your perception at the beginning, or did your perception begin to sway as I titled it?

_____
_____
_____
_____
_____
_____

3. Do you think it is possible to change your perception about something? Think of these two words: belief and perception. Do they have something in common? Belief is an acceptance that a statement is true or that something exists.

Perception is the ability to see, hear, or become aware of something through the senses.

_____
_____
_____
_____

4. Do you have a belief? Any belief that you feel strongly about? Would you like to share it? An example would be "I believe I am fat, I believe I am stupid".

_____
_____
_____
_____
_____
_____

5. Is this a rational belief or an irrational belief? Meaning does it make sense or not? List your beliefs, then next to them write if they are irrational or rational.

_____
_____
_____
_____
_____
_____

Can we challenge or change a belief? Let's see!

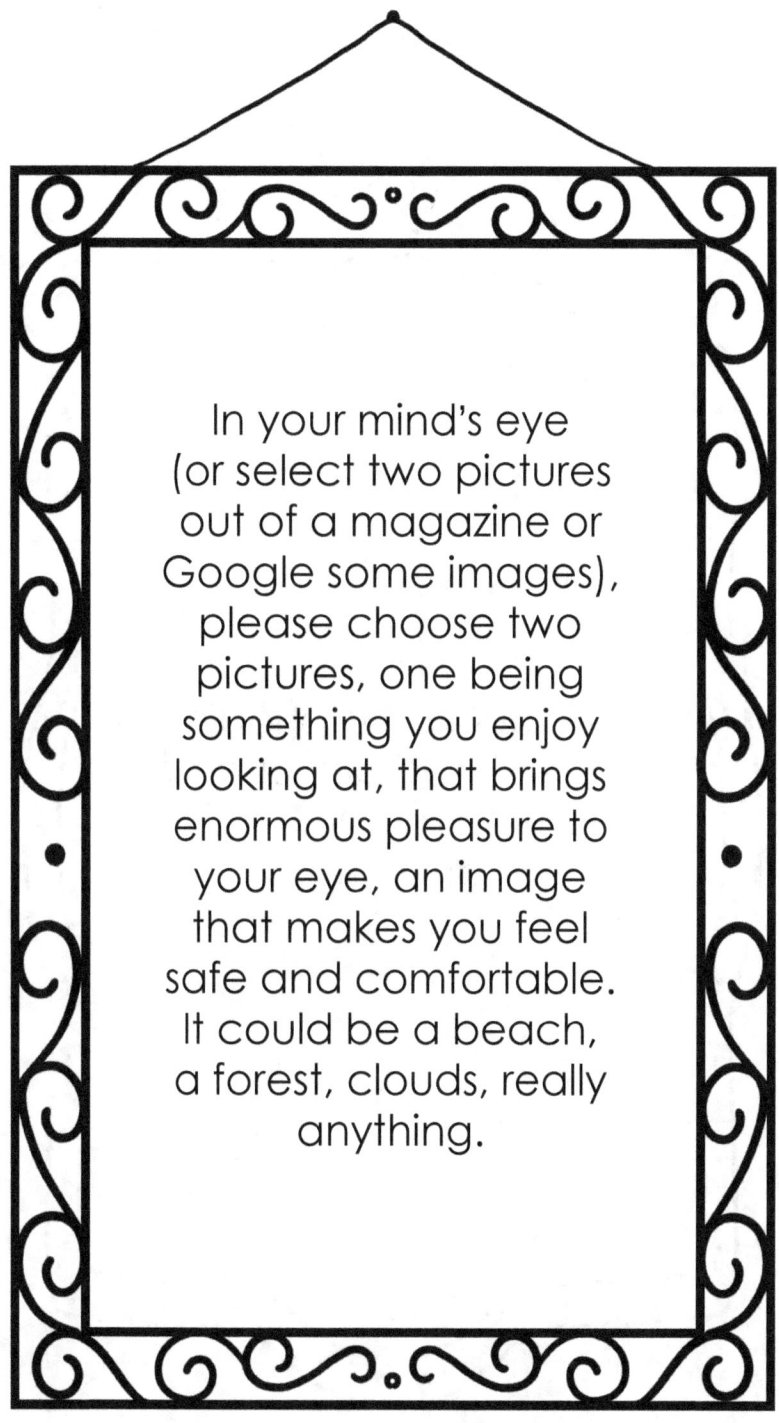

In your mind's eye (or select two pictures out of a magazine or Google some images), please choose two pictures, one being something you enjoy looking at, that brings enormous pleasure to your eye, an image that makes you feel safe and comfortable. It could be a beach, a forest, clouds, really anything.

For the next picture, choose something that really scares you. This could be something you have an opinion about or that causes your body and mind to react.

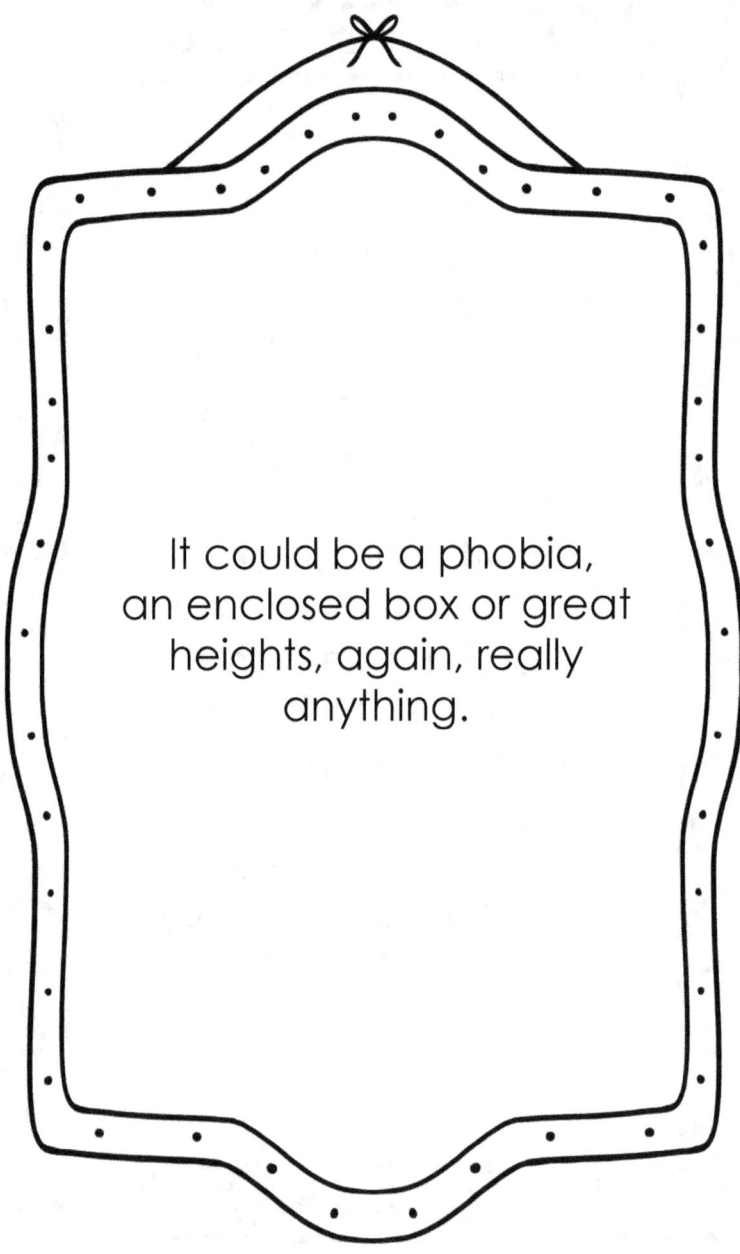

It could be a phobia, an enclosed box or great heights, again, really anything.

Next, take a moment to look at your positive picture and answer the following.

1. How do you feel emotionally looking at this picture? What emotions does it evoke?

_____

_____

2. How does your body feel? Can you feel the sensation of pleasure? Where in your body do you feel the sensation?

_____

_____

Now take a moment to look at your negative picture.

How do you feel emotionally looking at this picture? What emotions does it evoke?

_____

_____

How does your body feel? Can you feel the sensation of negativity? Where in your body do you feel the sensation?

_____

_____

Now put both pictures side by side in your mind's eye, or use the two physical copies of the images. Ask yourself, can you change the meaning of these images? If you titled them, would that change the meaning? What drew you towards choosing these pictures?

Now let's try something different. Let's see if you can change the meaning of these pictures. With scissors, glue and your imagination, make your negative picture positive, by integrating it into the positive picture. This creates a whole new third picture from the two you have!

1. How did you feel knowing you could cut the negative picture, taking it apart piece by piece and blending it into a positive image. Or are you finding it is leading you somewhere you never expected? Perhaps your picture is leaning towards being more negative?

_____
_____
_____
_____
_____

2. Place your new picture in front of you. How does it feel to know you had the ability to change the perception of the pictures? That you hold the power to create the outcome of both images?

_____
_____
_____
_____
_____

I was first asked to complete this activity during a trauma conference. My negative picture was of a small boy in a box, who I felt looked scared and could not breathe. I am claustrophobic, so this scared me. The young boy depicted my brother. My positive picture was the sky with birds flying freely. Polar opposites!

When they asked me to make the pictures blend into a positive picture, one was a trapped boy that I named *FEAR*; the other was an image of birds in the sky that I named *FREEDOM*.

Then I started to cut and paste. I freed the boy from the box and placed him in the sky flying with the birds. I kept the box, as it turned into a place of solitude and safety for the young boy. Essentially the fear was actually freedom from the big scary world we live in.

What causes our perception to be our own individual lens of the world? I'm often asked this question, yet it is extremely hard to put it into words. It falls under the category of, "How did you learn all this human interaction stuff"? But, honestly I don't know, it just came to me in a time of grief and trauma. Perhaps that's the correct answer.

After 9/11, my world was much different and not always to my liking. I came home, stood in front of my husband and said, "I am okay if you want a divorce," he looked at me bewildered, and I continued, "I am not me anymore. I am different and it's okay if you don't like the different me."

He straightened his head and smiled, " I love you more now, you are you. The real you, and I can't believe you are my wife."

My heart fell, and I felt a sigh of relief. My perception and beliefs about the world had changed greatly after aiding. I saw what evil exists, but I also saw what goodness humans have to give. I no longer worried about what I was eating at 5 p.m. for dinner. I no longer cared to look perfect or to keep up with the Joneses (who don't exist). I became real!

A mentor of mine, while I was aiding, would say, "Tomorrow, we get up, we mow our lawns as usual." I often had no idea what he was saying until I returned home. I woke up one Saturday and went outside and started my mower. Everything I did now seemed to come with great intention. I pulled the cord and heard the mower chug to start. As I pushed it along my lawn I saw the grass, the green, the bugs, the dirt; I saw life that I never saw before.

What affects our beliefs and our perceptions? Our experiences in life can have a massive impact. If we experience trauma or formulate a behavioural response as a child, we create and draw our perception and beliefs from it. Pavlov's conditioning experiment is a good example of this. Pavlov saw that, over time, if he rang a bell while feeding a dog, the animal knew to come and eat. Similarly, as children, we try out behaviours to see which one gets us the best results in particular circumstances.

Returning to our bottles of burdens, could they be responsible for our beliefs or perceptions of things? Chances are, yes. The things we experience in life do cause the mind, body and soul to create a perception or belief about oneself or the world. When you look at your bottle of burdens, ask yourself if they have caused you to see things differently now. Have they created or affected your beliefs and perceptions of things? As you saw, you have the ability to physically change the meaning of two pictures. Does this mean you would have the ability to change your perception of the world, if you addressed your burden within your bottle? I think YES!

CHAPTER FOUR: THE SCIENCE OF EMOTIONS

Emotions by far are the most challenging aspect of being human. When I am asked to speak about death in a school environment, most adults ask, "How do we handle the children's questions? What do we say? What do we do if someone cries or gets angry?"

When working with military families, often the veteran carries a lot of emotional baggage. Post-Traumatic Stress Disorder (PTSD) is often triggered by various things. So let's step back and ask ourselves why we are most fearful of the very thing that makes us human, our emotions.

Other animals do not express the same level of reasoning or emotion that we do as human beings. That being said, humans tend to shut down their emotions when it is of value to them. We are told, perhaps by societal norms, that we are not to express anger, and that we are not to express sadness. But, yet again, when grief or trauma hits humans, we have no choice but to show it all. The emotions are too heavy to bottle.

As we'll see in later chapters, our bottle will open or even break, at which point the naked human is free. Free to express, free to not care who hears them, to ignore all boundaries and utterly fall to their knees in emotion. What do those humans do? Some embrace, some run in fear, others judge, and some shut down.

I recall the moment that I woke up from surgery as a young girl. The doctor had nicknamed me Sunshine. I woke up to his words resonating through my body, "Sunshine, you don't have cancer. You have osteomyelitis, a rare bone infection found in old people. Sunshine, I want you to know one thing. If you don't talk about what is killing you on the inside, you will physically kill yourself. Your body can't take it." He then handed me a set of crutches that I used for many months. At the time I never really processed what he was talking about. I essentially added it to my full bottle (along with the death of my brother, a cancer scare, a learning disability and a negative body image).

As we've seen, we all have a bottle full of experiences or issues. An earlier behavioural task assignment (a simple activity) looked at how these burdens come into play in the development of your beliefs and perceptions. You were asked to explore your own perceptions and beliefs that were often derived from these experiences or burdens in the bottle.

Now I want you to take a closer look at how all this affects your physical being. You may be wondering what happens to the body when the bottle is full. Could your burdens, experiences and beliefs affect the body or cause some of your physical ailments? Let's try a little experiment.

THE SCIENCE OF EMOTIONS

Take a transparent glass and fill it with half vinegar and half water and then place it in front of you. Then take blue, red, green and yellow food colouring and match each colour with an emotion. Different cultures or people see different meanings for each colour. For example, blue can be seen as calm or sad, while red can be seen as anger or joy.

Now carefully pick up each colour and put a few drops of each into the glass. Be mindful while you do it, thinking of the colour and the emotions it carries for you. Give your emotions meaning and bring it to life.

As you drop in your colours ask yourself:

1. How does this colour relate to this emotion?
_____
_____

2. What does this colour represent in society?
_____
_____

3. Does this colour mean multiple things to you?
_____
_____

As you see all the colours swirling in the glass, ask yourself if the events from your past, or perhaps the unresolved issues contained in your bottle of burdens, have anything to do with the emotions you are expressing in your daily life. In other words, do your beliefs, your perceptions, have anything to do with the emotions swirling in the jar? Do you perhaps believe something, but are unsure as to why you believe it? Was there one colour you added more of which represented an emotion that you found particularly hard to either express or receive from others?

Now that you have expressed your emotions verbally and visually in the glass, please take a moment to ponder the following;

- **What colour is the water in the glass? Why is it that colour? (It is grey!!!)**
- **Can you relate the colour to your body physically?**
- **Can you relate it to your emotions and how you handle them?**
- **Do you feel you could change the colour of the water? How?**

When we don't express our emotions they must go somewhere. Where do you feel they go if we don't verbally express them or physically express them? The body carries muscle memory; would it not make sense that it carries much more than just a memory of muscle movement? What are your thoughts about the connection of your body to your emotions?

These are a lot of questions and a ton of realizations. (Welcome to the field of death and dying, where you learn everyday about yourself.) If you need to, you can pause before moving ahead with the rest of this activity.

Now I would like you to take a small amount of bleach and put it into your glass. Think of the bleach as your ability to express and wipe away your residue of emotions left from previous burdens, experiences or issues.

Asking yourself:
- **What colour is the water tuning?**
- **Why is that? (I know the chemical answer, which is, "Yellow, then to clear.")**
- **Think further into your being: why, when we express our emotions, does the water change colour?
How do you feel watching the colour change?**

Before we complete the answers let's look at emotions in another form. Bear with me, it may not be easy to look this closely at yourself. Again, it's okay to pause if needed.

Often in today's society we feel judgement for the expression of our emotions. Schools are now implementing coaching questions for negative and positive talk. They are trying various ways to help children identify each emotion. The most popular movie that is being used for this is called *Inside Out*. It depicts a young girl who has all these emotions in her head, and they talk to her. It is essentially as though she has a bottle in her head and does not share what is going on with anyone outside of her mind. The emotion-related characters argue, debate and decide what is the best way for the young girl to express or make life decisions. Of course she blows up in anger at the wrong times, as she explores positive and negative events that have created her perception and beliefs. She tries to challenge some of the negative events and to draw strength from the positive events. Ultimately, we watch as this young girl tries to make sense of it all, manipulating these emotions, until she too starts to feel overwhelmed (and grey, like the murky water in our activity). It isn't until she willingly lets go of the emotions and expresses them that the grey fog is lifted, and she feels clear inside.

    We are led to believe that emotions are something we can control at all times. We think we should always be able to express them in a polite and correct way. If we don't express them in the proper, socially acceptable way we are reprimanded. Which makes sense (we need to treat others and ourselves responsibly), but have we gone too far? Perhaps to the point that our understanding of emotions has been so suppressed that we now show no emotions until we burst?
    What if I were to tell you that emotions don't always make sense? What if I were to tell you that emotions don't follow a pattern? What if I were to tell you that an emotion can be triggered by a simple commercial on TV, if that taps into that memory bank? Let me give you an example of what emotions are really like.

PINWHEEL OF EMOTIONS

Envision a pinwheel. Then place the emotions that you identified with in the last activity on each point of the pinwheel. You may even add colour to each point of the pinwheel to reflect the previous activity with the water and food colouring. (For example, sadness is placed on one point of the pinwheel, and you colour it blue.) In the centre of the pinwheel put a label with your name on it.

Did it seem simple to make a pinwheel of emotions, even just in your mind's eye: Would this chapter be simple for someone who does not express well? Was it easy for you to identify emotions with colour? You may hear others say, as I often do, "This is stupid. Why would I do this childlike activity?" I often reply, "If it is childlike, why can't you do it?"

Is it so bad to act like a child or feel like a child again? Aren't most of our happiest memories from our childhood? Did we not create some of these emotions or beliefs in childhood? Would it not make sense to go back to our childhood to see what we derived from it?

The weather is not predictable. We do forecast what we think it may be like for the week. But sometimes a storm hits us from out of nowhere. Have you ever woken up wondering why you feel sad all day? Or perhaps you wake feeling happy or fulfilled? Then the next day you're the complete opposite?

Hold your pinwheel in front of you. Life is like the weather, some days it is calm and still, your pinwheel does not move at all. Perhaps your pinwheel stays stuck on one emotion all day. You may struggle all day with this one emotion. Or, the pinwheel may be spinning around and around, and you feel utterly crazy.

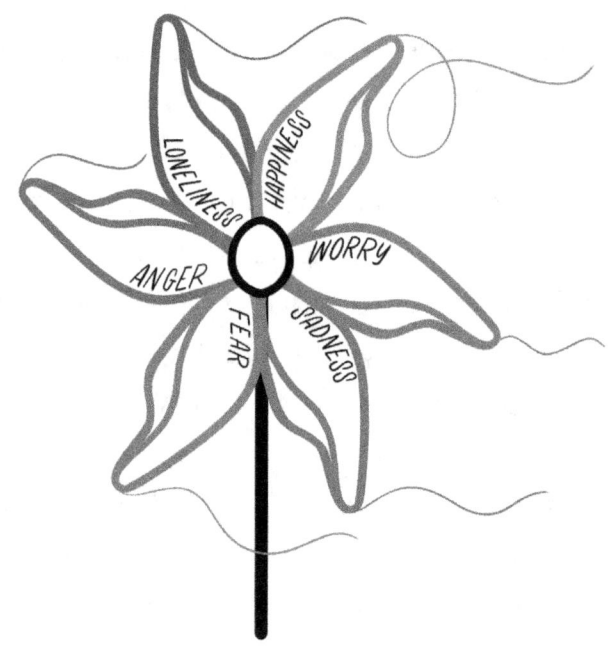

I am here to tell you that these experiences are normal. Can we expect to wake every day and feel amazing? There are so many other factors that play into how we feel. We must understand that emotions are not predictable, not the same for everyone, can change within minutes and can be expressed in so many ways. I hope that, so far, these activities or behavioural tasks have brought your emotions to life, so that you can see them, feel them and realize they exist!

CHAPTER FIVE: THE BODY'S EXPRESSION

Our body is a central component of ourselves, and it carries much more than we think. Not only does it hold our physical components, such as our organs, but it also carries our emotions, instincts, intuition and needs. I'd like you to guess the only emotional expression during which humans cannot control their body language.

You guessed it! It's my favourite area of study: grief.

During my time aiding others in the midst of world tragedies, I often observed body language. One family in particular had decided not to share with their children that their father had died in Afghanistan. Instead, they told the children that their father's deployment had been extended, and that he would be coming home after his duty was done. Working with these children, I was told to not disclose that their father was dead. I was instead supposed to help them with the grief of a missing father in their daily lives. The youngest child would often not speak, but I saw him observing me a lot. I noticed this behaviour was very prevalent, too, with his mother. He would watch your face and body intently as if to say, "I hear your words, but I read something different."

He eventually asked his mother directly, "Is dad dead?"

His mother replied, "No."

But, as she went on to explain that Dad was on extended deployment, her body language said something completely different. Her son, along with her other children, challenged her body language. They asked why she looked so sad, why her eyes said that their dad was dead. Eventually mom cracked and fell to her knees. She so badly wanted to protect her children from the horror of life. But instinctually, intuitively and emotionally the children knew her body was grieving.

I recently watched a documentary on body language. They explained body language so well, exploring how, before humans spoke, we had to depend on body language for survival. This essentially meant that our instincts had to be bang on. Because what if you approached another human, and they killed you? Or, what if you thought they were a friend, and they took all your food? Or, how would you ever know if someone wanted to mate?

In most cases people can lie to us with words. But, if we watch them closely, there are subtle clues that things are really not as the individual states. Even if a person *believes* a certain thing to be true (such as, "I am on a diet"), are those things really true?

Grief, being the only thing that humans cannot lie about, supports my theory that this emotion is the only non-discriminating equalizer of humans. The face has, for decades, made facial expressions that not only indicate emotions, but also help the body. For example, we scrunch our noses up when we smell something bad to protect our bodies. We innately put our feet towards people we are engaged with when standing near them. We naturally use body language to share how we feel without even knowing it.

Sometimes our bodies are speaking, and we can't hear them. A colleague mentioned working with a young boy who would never close doors, he resisted going into the washroom or any other small rooms. She asked that I work with him to see if we could address this behaviour. His father had died in the Twin Towers during the terrorist attacks. Exactly how his father died was vague.

As I worked with the boy, I noticed that he was nervous about sharing his feelings. It even seemed like he had entirely fallen into his bottle. There was no emotion, only more numbness. When I left a room we were in, I automatically closed the door. His response was intense; even though others were in the room with him, he lost it. He screamed as people came to his aid. I knelt down to the boy, "Look at me. Tell me what you see in your head? Let me help you through this."

His words crumbled the room to complete silence, "I was in the elevator with my dad. The door never opened."

My tears flow as I type this.

I grasped this young boy in my arms as he and the whole room sobbed. You see, he had a burden in his bottle that he could not verbalize, but his behaviour and belief of the door closing all resulted in his body speaking clearly. He was grieving.

 ## OUR LOVE IS INSEPARABLE

The next activity can have a huge impact on our bodies, and it involves Play-Doh. (I know… "Seriously?")

Please choose two pieces of Play-Doh that are different colours. Now take one colour, and only that colour, and mold it into something that represents YOU. This could be anything. If you love gardening perhaps a flower, or a football if you're a sports person or a pizza for a food lover. Anything that reflects you. Yes, create a representation of you with clay, give it a visual representation and bring it to reality. Now take the second colour, and only that colour, and mold it into a representation of someone or something that you love that has died. This could include pets, a marriage, a friendship or anything that has caused you enormous grief. Yes, create the GRIEF that is burdening you. Give it a visual representation and bring it to reality. It may be your present reality.

Now, put your creation of YOU and your creation of GRIEF side by side. Are there any similarities? Do they evoke similar emotions within you? (Again, this may evoke your emotions, so take a break if needed.)

Gently pick up your two creations in opposite hands. Hold them in front of you and slowly bring your hands together, combining your two creations. YOU and your GRIEF together! Smush, squeeze, blend, get your anger out and mix like crazy. (Some people make a whole new colour out of the two.) Now place the ball of mixed Play-Doh in front of you.

The next step is to try to separate the colours back to their original form. Take the two colours apart. Try hard, really hard? Is it possible? Can you? Why is that? Why can't you separate the colours? (A better question: Why do we in society separate body from mind?)

We can't separate the two pieces of Play-Doh because we can't separate you from a person you loved, perhaps someone who died, or from a marriage you loved for decades but that eventually ended, or from a friendship that you valued dearly.

I will always have similarities to my brother who died too young. My memories and the emotions I carry in my mind and body, in my heart, will forever be with me.

We can't separate our memories from our body or the physical effects they have on our bodies. We are one mind and body. So let's start blending the two together in order to live fully.

Living fully is not as easy as one may think. As we now know, emotions have to be expressed in some way. Like water, they always find a hole to flow through. A young family we will talk about next was working on anger, and they showed me clearly how the separation of one's burdens from one's mind does not always work.

The father of this young family experienced many outbursts of anger. He seemed to be tweaked by the sounds of young children. He was a veteran who had served in combat. When he returned home, his wife was excited for him to spend time with his children. He found quickly that his frustration level from the high pitched voices of the children resulted in him getting angry. His anger became very prevalent. He even tried to take the kids to a play group, at which point he ended up being escorted out as the noise raised him to a level of anger he could not control. His wife was contemplating filing for divorce. They both felt that this was a result of his time served in the military but saw no way to solve the problem.

While working with him, some major realizations that even I was not prepared for came flowing out of his bottle of burdens. Apparently, his job overseas was to set mines. One day, he set them in an area that looked vacant, but he noticed a round rock, or so he thought, some wood and other various objects that seemed like nothing. It turned out that the area was a playground. This realization not only brought him to tears, but me as well.

Once his wife understood and he understood, this burden that was well hidden, his life became a little less angry and more compassionate. Words are hard to come by when dealing with such traumatic emotional experiences. This family is a clear example of how anger is not always anger. What we express is not always what we would choose to express.

CHAPTER SIX: WHAT MASKS DO YOU WEAR?

It took years to realize that I was living in a bottle. Essentially, this bottle had become my safe zone. You could even look at it as a mask that I could put on and take off when I needed to.

When I was pregnant with my second child, I was extremely excited to share the news with my Nan, who was the mother of eight children. I would visit her every Thursday with my son, Jacob. He was only two and loved the watermelon that Nan would get for him. When I think back on these times, life seemed almost perfect. Jacob also wore clothes that Nan taught me how to sew, and he'd play by her pond while we sat watching and sipping our cups of tea on sunny days.

To me, Nan was an amazing woman and was always my biggest cheerleader. She would dress up and come meet me at work for lunch. She adored me, and I could feel that love resonate from her. She would never shake my bottle or the reality I created for myself. It was a perfect world to me.

Eventually, Nan reached the end of her life. After one of our Thursday visits, I stood over Nan's hospital bed as she whispered, just before she fell deep into a coma. Nan was coming to the reality of her own death as she spoke softly to me saying, "I will say hello to Robert."

I brought my head up and replied, "Robert?"

She then reached for my hand, "Chrissy, Robert is your dead brother."

My knees buckled and my heart fell as my bottle smashed to pieces at my feet. I could feel the glass digging into the soles of my feet as I processed the fact that I was living in a bottle of trauma that I never felt or accepted. I stepped back from the bed as my family returned to be by her side while Nan slipped away. I stood leaning against an old radiator as memories rushed into my mind. I could see red... I could feel red, I could see my family standing over my brother's grave. My mind was flooded with memories. My aunt asked me if I was okay. "Yes," I replied, and slowly walked down the hall as sensations filled my body for the first time in decades.

This realization took me on a journey I could have only dreamt of. One that forced me to look at the reality of my life. I had to start with figuring out what and where Robert was. (This journey resulted in the creation of my first book, *Where is Robert?*, which aided more than 6,000 families affected by the September 11 attacks. It also launched my career into the field of grief and personally changed my perspective on a lot of things.)

Belief modification became the norm for me, as I saw myself challenging every belief I had, good or bad. I created or became the me I wanted to be, the authentic, true me. With that discovery came the acceptance of many of my idiosyncrasies. At this time, I also began to accept that I had a disability (according to the school system) affecting the comprehension of words called "dyslexia". This, in turn, caused me to read body language over listening to the spoken word.

My dyslexia made it harder for me to comprehend what people were trying to say to me, so I would fill in the blanks with their body language. I slowly noticed that I verbalized the things most individual's thought but would never say. And with that came the realization that my discussion of "the elephant in the room" was not socially acceptable. Someone once said, "What audacity you have." I had no idea how to respond to that; I did not know if it was an insult or compliment. But I knew the person saying it greatly loved me, so I smiled in response and went home and looked the word up. The definition was "a willingness to take bold risks". (I rather giggled.) It does take audacity to look inwards at yourself emotionally, and to look at others and to expect the same from them.

During my journey to connect my body, emotions, instincts and intuition with my conscious self, I observed something else that, oddly enough, really bothered me. I was a fashion model for years, and as a six-foot redhead I was a rarity to find in the industry. I was able to create a niche for myself. I could carry wedding gowns that many could not. I truly loved fashion and the many ways it allows us to change and experiment with our appearance. During my modelling years I also became a hairdresser who loved to do avant-garde extreme hair styles. I even created a number of hats out of hair.

Yet through all this I felt like an imposter. I was not

as beautiful as everyone had thought, or so I would say to myself. *I have tricked them all.* I was hiding a physical secret. They saw a beautiful woman whom they felt was born that way. I knew that I had an A-cup on the left side and a D-cup on the right. (You can only imagine how hard that was to hide!) I wanted so badly to share my secret with the world, so they, too, could realize that no one is perfect.

In today's society, Facebook, Twitter, LinkedIn and many more social media crazes have taken over our identity. In a way, haven't they become the many masks we wear? We can create and mold this mask, or rather our avatar, our identity, in whatever way we wish the public to perceive us. We can take photos and alter them to our liking. We can post phrases or pictures that depict us as we want to be seen. But are we really posting information that is about us? Or are we posting information about the person we wish to become?

Have you ever really listened to people? When an individual's phrase begins with, "I am _____ (a non-smoker, a very positive person).", but their actions do not match what they are saying, don't you ever start to wonder why that person even said that? On social media you will see someone post the most amazing adventures, and other people are liking and commenting like crazy about how jealous they are. Yet if you meet that friend for lunch, they complain about how awful life has been. Are you not totally confused?

And yet how is this different from me hiding my disabilities, both educationally and physically? Should I have posted all about them? Or should I have kept them private? Or is this more a personal choice?

My experience as a model, having to keep personal details hidden, sparked my research on my undeveloped left breast. While researching breast surgery I realized that I had quite a few options (such as surgically moving tissue from one area to another or receiving an implant). But, during this era, there were many societal opinions such as, "Accept what you were given," or, "Be with someone who loves you as you are." On the opposite end there were others: "I would totally go for it!', or "Free boob job. You are so lucky!"

My research took years to complete, and finding a plastic surgeon was not easy. I did find a support group of ladies who had had experiences with bad implants, and who met up weekly in Toronto. I took a leap of faith and attended one of their meetings. As I walked down a flight of stairs in this rather unique, seventies-style home, I saw a few chairs empty in the circle. I listened and watched as each lady shared what brought them to the meeting. Most had received horrible implants. Some had faced the challenge of breast cancer. But, there existed one commonality between the women: they all talked very highly of Women's College in Toronto. One doctor in particular was often mentioned.

As I drove home from Toronto, tears flowed down my cheeks, filling my lips with a salty taste. My tears were for a different reason this time, for the first time in what felt like forever. I cried with relief, knowing that I was not alone in this journey.

I am sure you've guessed what I did next. The very first thing the next morning, I made a call to Women's College. I got my appointment six months later, and now I have balanced, beautiful boobs!

Do you wear a mask? Is the mask just hiding a burden (in my case, an imbalanced breast)? This can be a hard question to answer or explore. What would happen if you tore off all the layers of your mask? Would that be wise? Would it have been wise for me to share my personal details with the world?

Let's look at it in a different perspective, going back to, "What came first, the egg or the shell?" (No, not the chicken.) Was the shell first formed before the slimy egg inside? The essence and emotions of the egg are not the shell, but what's inside. The reason the egg exists isn't *because of* the shell. If there weren't any life inside, there would be no need for the shell.

Learning to recognize that your shell is different from your essence and emotions is important. You are the life mass inside. Although the shell, or mask, protects you in some situations, it is ineffective—or worse—in other situations. There are times to use your masks and times to shed them. Take a moment and ask yourself the following questions:

1. **When should the mask you carry that protects your essence and emotions be up and on alert? Be specific.**
2. **Then think about the instances when you should shed your mask and keep it off. Be specific.**

When we hear the phrase, "You're wearing a mask", it feels negative. But is it? Various cultures have used masks for healing, connecting, entertainment, inspiration etc. Masks give us the ability to connect without revealing our essence and emotions, or our true being all the time. Sometimes it is better to wear our mask for our own safety or self-preservation. This is perhaps why so many people on social media create masks: to protect themselves from the reality of their true lives. Or perhaps they simply don't want to share their essence and emotions on that platform. In this sense, masks exist everywhere, both with positive and negative impacts.

During a grief camp for teenagers, I used a mask-making activity to help teens express the emotions they were unable to express verbally. The grief was often too heavy to express. During that week, a young man, who was identified as having every syndrome imaginable, was a challenge. As I walked around the table during our sessions he would put his foot out to trip me. He always had a funny comment and a great laugh.

One day during a discussion of a heavy topic, the young man made a joke that caused the room to become silent. I turned to this young man and said, "I know what you're doing. I do it too."

He stopped, rather stunned, and said, "What?"

I replied, " I, too, use laughter to change the atmosphere or the mood. If I can't handle it, I change the focus to me."

He slowly deflated in his chair as I continued, "That's actually a gift you have, and it's not being utilized. Let's use it."

As the teen quickly straightened in his chair, filled with excitement, the group giggled at his reaction.

By the end of the week this young man created the most amazing mask from red and black feathers, and with great trepidation on my part he took to the stage. He did an amazing job showing how 9/11 affected his world. After the performance, he explained how the black over the mouth of the mask represented that he was not allowed to express his anger. The black over the top of the head of the mask was society capping his abilities to express himself. This mask gave this young man the ability to express himself for the first time in an effective, impactful way.

Now I'd like you to look at your own use of social media. Let's start with Facebook. If you didn't know yourself, how would you perceive yourself based on that medium? If you're really daring, ask a friend, or someone who does not know you well, to give their opinion of your life. (I was recently at a funeral, and someone came up to me and said, " I only ever see you on Facebook getting awards and travelling the world." I was kind of shocked and thought, *Wow, is that the mask I have created?)*

Next, look at another social media site, such as LinkedIn. Here they are asking you to share or create a different mask from the one that is shown on Facebook. This is more of a career or business mask. Perhaps your career *causes* you to wear a mask. Again, not all masks are negative.

Here are some other tough questions:

On social media, do you feel you have portrayed yourself fully?
Or, do you believe that we should portray ourselves fully on these sites?
Who are the people on your social media?
Why are you sharing with them?
Is it for your own needs or theirs?
Have you ever taken time away from social media?
If yes, why?
Why do you think people take time away from social media?

I myself have taken some time away from these activities. I call this my "S.S." or social media sabbaticals. I found that I don't miss it as much as I thought I would. Honestly, my brain feels lighter. The realization that we have an electronic mask that, at times, we can walk away from or use to our advantage, is all okay. Everything can be done in moderation and within balance for our emotional, physical and soul health.

As the young man at the grief camp discovered, to bring a mask to life is quite an experience! A mask can be created from anything. You can use already formed masks, or start with paper, wood or aluminum foil. The quickest option is to start with an already formed mask, which can be found at any craft store. Now, think about how you feel society sees you. Next, create a mask that you feel reflects this. While creating your mask, use colour and texture, keeping in mind how others perceive you daily.

Create something that says, "This is how I feel people see me." For example, the first time I did this, my mask looked wild. It had red hair and had lots of colour, but over my lips I put a butterfly, because it represents death and new life. The placement of the butterfly represented my belief that society didn't want to hear me talk about the subject of death and had tried to silence me. Create something that touches you deeply. This could be a passion you have that is seen by many.

The next step is to make the *inside* of the mask a projection of how we would like to be perceived.

Once your mask is complete, put it to your face. (Sounds weird, but try it on and see how it feels.) Does it make you feel comfortable? Safe? Often masks give us the ability to share more with others. As you remove the mask, look inside it to the part that was touching your face. What would you like the mask to look like to *others*? How would you like them to see your authentic self or true insides?

During the creation of my mask, I became agitated as a very masculine policeman next to me was a creating monster. He was making this amazing mask with so much colour and with precise lines. I started to feel and hear the words, "You can't do this. You have never been crafty at all." I started to feel my body respond to my words. I was beginning to deflate. Just then we were asked to place the masks on. In my head, I was thinking, *Seriously?* The masculine policeman looked over at me with a funny grin as he placed his mask on. As I looked into the white of the back of the mask, I heard the words, "What would you like to project to the world?"

I painted the whole inside in blue swirls. I wanted the world to see the calm me, the me who didn't cause fear in others when discussing death. I wanted and still do want others to realize that looking at grief in all its forms brought me peace, as crazy as that sounds …

CHAPTER SEVEN:
THE GIFT OF "THE SEEING"

Connecting to people is one of the strangest experiences in life. Some you walk up to and immediately feel comfortable with. You may have not even spoken to them yet, but you automatically feel comfortable in their presence. I am still learning even at my age, nearing fifty, that the knowledge I carry many others don't, and the knowledge others carry I know nothing about. What am I really saying? That we don't know much about each other at all.

The only way to truly get to know people is to connect with them on a level where they feel comfortable showing the real them. No barriers or masks or bottles to protect themselves. But how do you get there, one may ask? Is this something you can force? Does it take time to connect with others?

In my work, due to the fact grief is so impacting to the human body, mind and spirit, I often get to see the real sides of people, as the grief has taken away all masks and barriers and shattered all bottles. I have a window of time to truly connect with these people, and that's when I do my job. I coach them through those tough emotions, helping them to understand the physical reactions that accompany the enormous pain they are experiencing.

The first step to connecting properly with another human is being able to connect with ourselves. You may say, "Well, I am in this body, so I am pretty connected." Are you really? So many times I have seen people living in their bottles, as I did, without actually breaking out, or wanting to break out. It is safe and comfortable, and after a while they believe that is all there is in life, and they become content with that.

While at a bereavement conference, I was asked to present the Helping Children Understand Grief Sessions (HUGS) Program. I was also able to attend the other workshops. During a workshop, the instructor asked us to connect with a part of our bodies. We had a brief mediation before we started to draw out these parts of our bodies. Now I should back up. Most attendees were academics, and it was a huge honour to be presenting alongside them. The instructor kept emphasizing to get into our bodies, and I began struggling with this, as I was already heavily into my body. Essentially, I wanted to be in my mind, just like everyone else in the room. I had never been able to understand my mind fully, as I was taught not to trust my mind, and that it was backwards and dyslexic. Finally, as we neared the end of the mediation she said go where we felt the strongest pull. For me, that was definitely my mind.

As I opened my eyes, she instructed us to start to draw what we saw and felt with colourful pastel crayons. I started with the yellow pastel and started to smear this colour out onto the paper. Then I picked up orange and did the same. I was so immersed in the project that I didn't even notice the others around me. I was pushing so hard with my pastels that the dust was all over the table, floor and my hands. Last, I picked up a baby blue pastel and made two wings, and then blended them into the yellow and orange.

As I slowed my hands down and was able to clearly see what I drew, my tears began to flow. I sat staring at this picture, knowing that I had been there before. I had felt this calmness often, as I had envisioned this imagine in a time that I needed to feel comfort and trust. My tears started to drip onto the picture, blending the colours even more, as I came to the realization that my mind is part of my body. Who knew my mind was part of my being, body and whole self? I had always separated my mind from my body.

As I sat there I heard the instructor say, "Your picture is interesting. Do you want to share?"

As I raised and looked around, noticing that most participants had drawn pictures of items, a house or a heart, and also that everyone's hands were pretty clean. I couldn't hold back my tears and explained that I had never trusted my mind, and that the realization that my mind is part of my whole being had really hit me. I shared my picture of a bird flying into a beautiful sunset, because this is what my mind sees and feels. I feel freedom to be who I am.

The instructor's next words were very impactful:" You have the gift of the seeing."

I stopped for a second and could feel all eyes on me. I wondered as to why she said that? I replied, "Yes I do."

Afterwards I asked my colleagues if I had said anything about the gift of the seeing. They all replied, "No, but it's obvious." I thought, *Really????*

As I was leaving the large hall the instructor came

running after me to say thank you. Many of the participants had approached her asking "What was that all about?", and, "What is the seeing?"

Looking further back, I recall the first time that I truly believed in the gift of "the seeing", as the instructor called it. I was aiding at an old dude ranch that was converted into a place for children to stay during their last stages of illness. Nestled in the woods, it was this amazing facility. It had been renovated to accommodate what nurses and doctors needed to administer medication along with other requirements for palliative care. But at that time, we were using it to run our grief camps.

When I arrived at the camp I was truly amazed at what this area in New York had accomplished in a place full of nature. I even recall seeing a donkey who wandered around, often visiting the mini hospital as the children were being checked out. We all stayed in cabins of our own, and in mine, beautiful stained wood adorned the fireplace. My bed was completely made of huge pieces of actual trees. It was such an unreal experience to fully connect with nature.

One night early on I was having trouble sleeping. I opened the top drawer of the dresser next to my bed and found a journal. This journal was already full of stories from others who had slept in the same bed. It was fascinating to read these stories of how some came for a small length of time and others actually stayed here as they watched their children take their last breaths. As I turned the pages, I began to cry. All these individuals, despite their different handwriting were connected by the similar pain they shared.

During my long hours of work, I would often lose inspiration or sight of what I was supposed to be doing for these young children. Day in and day out, we all could feel the heaviness of grief. We would hike mountains; we would canoe; we would create masks; we would eat, clean, and play games; but the heaviness of grief always remained. I started to lose confidence that I was even capable of helping these children. Most nights I was able to sleep, but that one night was different.

Since we didn't have a cell phone signal, I decided to go for a walk. As I wrapped myself in a blanket, I stepped out of the cabin and into the silence of the woods. I could hear the ground crunch under my feet as I walked silently towards a kaleidoscope of light. As I listened to the woods speak, I was intrigued by what was creating this beautiful light that I saw off in the distance. I walked towards it and came upon an old chapel. I stood in front of the chapel amazed at its beauty. I slowly shuffled up the stairs and turned the door knob; it creaked as it opened. I walked towards the tiny altar and saw the beauty of the stained-glass windows in front of me. My heart pounded as I wondered, *Should I be here?*

That's when I noticed an apple sitting on the stair of the altar. I picked it up, and as I stood my eyes were drawn to an open book in front of me. As my eyes glanced over the words I saw one phrase was circled, "Words fitly spoken are like apples of gold in pictures of silver." As I read this, I looked down at the apple in my hands. *You knew I was coming?* I heard voices that jolted me out of my thoughts. When I looked up, I saw a chapel full of people. My eyes widened as I braced myself, thinking that I just went insane. I walked towards the pews that were full of so many different cultures, clothing, colours and songs. I admitted to myself that I was working way too much.

I sat in amazement as I listened to the singing and the hum of the piano behind me as it started to accompany the voices. I watched as these people filled me with an amazing amount of love that I had never experienced in my life, a feeling that will never leave me. (As often happens in my work, my tears flowed.)

I woke on a pew to the sun gleaming in my eyes and an apple tucked into my blanket. I stood up slowly, wondering if I was alone. I quickly grabbed my blanket and apple, and swiftly moved towards the door, needing to prep my class for the day. As I swung the door open I heard the sound of digging. I looked sideways to a man who was shovelling a small hole in the graveyard that adorned the side of the chapel. He looked at me with a smile and said, "Wow, you can play the piano beautifully." I stood stunned by his words. Excuse me? He continued saying, "That is an amazing gift you have."

I knew I was late for class, but I grabbed my blanket even tighter and replied, "If you only knew, sir."

The next day had fallen on the second to last day of camp, which was the day I asked each participant to bring in a photo of the significant individual who had died in the Twin Towers (this group was primarily from New York). I asked each child to share about their loved one who had died with the group. As they started to pin photos of their loved ones onto a large banner, I started to feel my knees weaken. I slowly sat down next to a volunteer who had not lost anyone in the Towers that day.

As the children showed their picture and shared their stories, my body became encompassed in the realization that love extends beyond this universe. I slowly realized that the pictures were the people in the chapel that I had seen the night before. Their families came to me to be a guide, and to help me help these children.

Seeing my face, a volunteer placed her hand on my knee, saying, "I have no idea why I am here. I just know I was to come and help. Oddly enough, I have been placing apples in the chapel as it felt like the right thing to do." I was amazed. I felt everyone's eyes look at me. We all embraced each other as I said, " I get it: words fitly spoken are like apples of gold in pictures of silver. When we follow our hearts, the words will come that need to be said."

CHAPTER EIGHT:
ARE WE CREATING OUR OWN REFLECTIONS?

We've all heard expressions such as, "Mirrors don't lie", or, "The world is your mirror", or "Mirrors show us what we look like, not who we are". But could our environment also be a mirrored reflection of ourselves?

An old Japanese folktale might help. A happy dog bounces, with his tail wagging and ears up high, into a fun house that is full of mirrors. He looks into the mirror and sees 100 other happy dogs looking just as joyful staring back at him. He feels the warmth and friendship of them all. He walks out thinking to himself, *This is a great place. I will come back and visit it often.* In the same village another little dog, who was not quite as happy as the first one, decided to visit the house. He slowly climbed the stairs with his head hung low as he looked into the door. When he saw the 100 unfriendly dogs looking back at him, he growled at them and was horrified to see 100 little dogs growling back at him. As he left he thought to himself, *That is an awful place, and I will never go back there again.*

The little dogs created their own atmosphere in the funhouse of mirrors. Their experience was based on their body language, emotional state, perception and the mask they chose to wear that day. When you understand that the world is your mirror, you can focus your camera lens inward, rather than outward, and observe.

It is hard to fathom the idea that we have the ability to mold our environments to make them as wonderful as we want them to be (perhaps fancy houses, the best decorated home, with gardens of beautiful flowers). Many clients talk about their houses and homes not being as they'd like. Most will say that the house is messy and unorganized, and this was not how they had expected their living environments to be. One person, who felt the opposite, was obsessed with things being perfect in her home. She spent endless hours debating with her husband on how to make the decor match on opposite sides of the room. She truly believed that her curtains did not match each other. No matter what anyone else said ("The light reflecting from the window could be causing the difference," or, "Could different light content hitting the room cause a colour difference?"), she held firmly to her opinion that they did not match, but should match, perfectly. During this time she also struggled with many relationships. Fifth marriage, butting heads with a teenage son, trying to advance in her career, and so on, ultimately unfulfilled with where she was in life.

I began to question whether her obsession with the curtains was a reflection of how imperfect her life seemed. Could a pristine home be a reflection of what she wanted in herself, perfection to "keep up with the Joneses"? After many years of denial, anger and much self-reflection, she came to the realization that the curtains were not different shades; essentially, it was the lens she was looking through that made the shade different. When she moved this obsession inward, she then saw the different shades within herself.

She had spent many years in counselling to no avail, but she had a great understanding of why she was behaving this way, it wasn't until she reached out consciously to connect with her body and mind, that her bottle of burdens opened. She took each burden or fear and addressed it head on with activities (behavioural tasks) to release the burden from her reactive unconscious mind. This process caused her wise conscious mind to kick in and to create some new, rational beliefs and perceptions. Her relationships mended and grew as she did. Her home became a little less perfect and a little more inviting. She realized that it didn't really matter if the light caused the curtains to be slightly different, as long as she was happily sitting on the couch next to her son and husband. The differences in the curtains were actually very pretty.

Are our environments created by us? Another client was the complete opposite of the woman in the previous story. He was more the norm. When we met he said, "I am a minimalist." Yet as I entered his home, I didn't see minimalism (nor did it matter to me). I saw his fear of judgement. Then he explained that his house was too small for his liking and lifestyle, which I could understand for the two people living there with a large dog. As with my other client, his home was (maybe) a reflection of their relationship. Funnily enough, *both* clients became angry at me when I pointed this out to them. Both made excuses and said, "No, not at all."

Another client, whose home felt very warm and

welcoming, was much different than the last. The only thing I noticed was that it was very incomplete. It looked like it had halted at a stage of development. As I worked with this young man, his relationships were at the same stage. The loss of his parents had impacted him more than he let on. Essentially, he bottled up and halted the grieving process.

Sometimes these delays are unavoidable. Once, at a hospice conference, a colleague said, "My father died last month. Don't give me that look. I don't want to cry. I am not grieving until the end of the year. I don't have time to grieve." I respected her wishes and said, " You know where I am." People have the ability not only to halt pain, but to displace it. As a professional, she clearly knew she had this ability, and my questioning may have lifted the lid off her bottle just a bit. We could *not* have that happen at a conference.

Eventually the young man stuck with it; he opened the bottle, removed the masks, and accepted who he truly was. As he evolved, his home evolved, too, into a completed project. His relationships started to shift and to intertwine in a healthy manner, and his relationship with his partner became fulfilling. He realized that the clutter and incomplete home was a reflection of his own mind. He shared how he had felt that he never completed anything in life. When he finally completed the renovations on his home, with his husband by his side, they both felt the joy of a clutter-free environment, mind and relationship.

The hardest thing for any human being to do is consciously connect with oneself. We fear what we don't know. Looking in the mirror can be scary, as we may not know the next step we are supposed to take. It is not what happens to us but how we handle it that creates who we are. When I awake, for example, I usually sit in bed thinking about the day ahead. If I know it is going to be rough, I can think about upcoming events, and my body will react accordingly. I can start to cry from sadness or begin to tighten up in anxiety. If I recall an event from the past, my body will respond the same way, according to the emotions that are evoked from the memory.

THE MIRROR OF YOUR MEMORIES

This next activity is challenging, so take care of yourself as you need to. What's in the mirror of your mind's memory?

Take a moment while looking in the mirror and relax your body in a chair. Make sure to connect with yourself visually using your eyes.

- Take three deep breaths watching yourself inhale and exhale. Keeping the connection with your eyes.
- Now slowly close your eyes and trust it is okay, you're watching yourself in the mirror with your eyes closed… slowly bring forth a happy memory (this can be done with a sad memory, but I would suggest doing that with someone, not alone).
- Sit with the happy memory, and see it clearly in your mind's eye.
- Look at the people you're with, who they are, their body language and expressions. Are they laughing? Are you attached to these people emotionally? Physically? Sit for as long as you need to explore this memory.

When you feel ready slowly open your eyes to see your reflection in the mirror and answer the following questions.

Who was in your memory?
_____
_____
_____

What was their body language saying to you?
_____
_____
_____

What was their emotional expression saying to you?
_____
_____
_____

Is this person or people still an active part of your life?
_____
_____
_____

Do you want to keep this person in your life? Even as a memory? Meaning, for example, that if someone has passed on, do you want to carry this memory or event with you now?
_____
_____
_____

The last question is especially relevant when you're bringing forth a negative memory. Do you want to keep this person in your life? (Know that there is a step for letting go of toxic relationships and doing it in a way that is healthy for both parties.)

We will explore that later.

This activity using a happy memory reveals how much of a connection you have with your emotional responses to memories and past events. One thing is for sure: memories can hide from us. Our amazing mechanism of emotional denial or bottle burdens can take a memory and delete it or change it to fit our mirror image. Practicing this activity allows the mind to make space for older memories to come forth and be explored. This is a great way to learn about your behaviours and perhaps why you do them!

Post-Traumatic Stress Disorder has become very well known for at least the last decade. Often people believe that this term applies only to veterans. While they are more often the ones with the most extreme or most visible cases, in our own lives, we encounter PTSD more often than we realize. PTSD shows up when a terrifying memory or event is triggered by something and, often, the individual had no idea that the memory existed.

You can probably see the connection to the bottle of burdens and hidden memories within our minds. After fifteen years of aiding, I was at a "Mom and Me" group at the local school. (I had decided at forty to have another child, realizing that motherhood was, by far, my best career choice.) The children and caregivers were all outside playing in the sun. The town next to us, Niagara-On-The-Lake, had announced weeks earlier that they were opening our first local airport for smaller commercial planes. While playing a game with the children, I heard the loud roar of a plane, and the feeling of the ground as it started to rattle. Instantly, without hesitation or consciously knowing (perhaps it was my reactive unconscious mind dictating what to do), I started to round the children up, feeling that I had to get the children inside to safety.

Panicking, I felt another mother's hand on my shoulder, while she was saying, "Christine, Christine."

Her touch jolted me out of my perceived situation. When I looked up I saw a passenger plane flying overhead, and when I looked sideways, I could smell the freshly cut grass from a large riding lawn mower. These two things together triggered a memory that evoked a bodily reaction. I realized that, when aiding, we were trained in what to do when an attack happens. I sat down, not being able to share my thoughts, and simply said, "Wow, that plane really scared me." No one questioned my behaviour, but I sensed that they were talking about it.

Coming to the realization that a burden, event or experience creates a memory that can have a lasting impact on us is a challenge. Acceptance of the fact we were traumatized or impacted by something bigger than our awareness is hard to accept. But, an even tougher challenge is to realize that you can *change* the impact on yourself and move beyond it. Like my clients, I had to realize that,"It takes courage to live life." In contrast, it is easy to go through the movements of life (work, play, mow the lawn, sleep), but to *live* it? Now that takes courage. Living life means feeling life fully, consciously connecting to everything and consciously disconnecting from the things we don't need.

    We have all perfected disconnecting, because the body and mind have mechanisms that don't like pain. Physically, if something hurts us, we run or move away from it. The bottle for that pain is our emotional denial. When something emotionally hurts us the mind says, "Put it away in the bottle and seal it tight." As the two clients who didn't realize that their homes reflected their bottles of burdens, I didn't realize that my PTSD even existed until my body physically reacted at the moms group. It took great courage, on my clients part and mine, to consciously stay in the game of life.

CHAPTER NINE: CUTTING THE CORD

Research on PTSD in the world of arts and healing includes treatment through exposure therapy. But that can also have adverse effects, and can even end up re-traumatizing an individual. So it is not taken lightly and needs to be approached cautiously, drawing on professional support. In my own healing journey, I exposed myself to my fears slowly, and I was able to move forward.

A coaching session summed up these experiences. Debriefings with colleagues while aiding, I recalled all the horrors I had witnessed. I cried and slept for days. I slowly motivated myself back to a place of functioning, only to have a coach lay out my problems on a plate. After a few hours of discussion, my coach said, "Let me rephrase this for you: your fear to become fully what you're meant to be, a professional speaker, writer and coach in the field of trauma and grief, is it based on plausibility?" He had taken my fear of the big, bad monster, otherwise known as a terrorist, down to one word. What are the chances? Is it plausible? This was otherwise known as a fear of the unexpected.

So how the heck do we get out of this mindset that the big, bad, scary monster may return? Was I, like my clients, creating my own reflection in my environment? What was the solution to this fear exposure therapy? Monthly, I jumped on the stage with sweaty palms, my heart racing ninety miles an hour and slowly I came to the realization that I was "the real deal", that I practice what I preach. I soon learned that "I am who I want to be", and that my success was always a balancing act. I still have to revisit my bottle frequently to help ease my fear that the "bad people" may come again.

Even with this foundation for success, I was stuck pondering the word "plausibility". Did I set up my own roadblocks? Also, I was then thirty pounds heavier. And I seemed to talk myself out of submitting manuscripts to agencies and was even reluctant to propose speaking engagements. Seeing this behaviour in myself, I decided to try to cut the cord of connection to this word "plausibility".

As with our other activities, the next visual journey may be difficult, and it may take daily or weekly practice. When we look in the mirror, we see that our emotions and body are interconnected, meaning that one reacts to the other. Our memories can evoke emotional reactions, the same way that physical pain can evoke an emotional reaction or vice versa. For instance, do you ever think of a memory so painful that you feel it all over your whole body, perhaps a sensation like goose bumps, or your chest even begins to hurt? If we react both physically and emotionally to the memory of an event or trauma, can we have control over the reactions we give to those memories? What if we could remove our emotional and physical reactions to those memories?

CUTTING THE CORD OF CONNECTION

This activity includes several steps. Take your time.

1. You may use a mirror, as in the previous chapter, if it helps you to stay focused. Connect with your eyes in the mirror.
2. Take three deep breaths keeping the connection with your eyes in the mirror. As you practice over time you may be able to do this without the mirror, it will come naturally to you.
3. Slowly close your eyes and trust yourself.
4. Bring forth a memory, and slowly visualize the memory.
5. Now walk through the memory. Interact with the memory *as you wish to*.
6. Allow your body to feel the sensations that you felt when living in this moment. If the emotions become too much to handle, remind yourself that you are in control, that this is only a memory. If feelings are too intense, try touching something or moving your body to ground yourself back to your environment. This will give a feeling of safety to the mind and body.
7. When you're grounded and feel safe, dive back into the memory. Look at the people within the memory, look at the environment, describe the people and the

environment out loud, if you need to.

8. Connect your emotions to the memory, the people and the environment. For example, if you are sitting on a bench with your family members, feel the emotions you would as if this was all real.

9. Now when you are ready, create a cord. Visualize and feel a cord streaming from you to your memory. This cord can connect to people in the memory, the environment or the emotions it evokes. (My cord connected to the Twin Towers, because they represent the word "plausibility" in my mind.)

10. See the cord in your mind's eye. See how it has you connected both physically and emotionally to this memory. See how this cord has you connected to the people in this memory. Finally, see who or what the cord has you connected too emotionally in this memory. Ask yourself, how does this cord and its connections to this memory make me feel? How do these connections impact your daily emotions?

11. Now, only when you're ready, I want you too slowly, when you feel ready and only when you feel ready, release and cut the cord. Release the cord of connection to this memory. Some may see the cord dissolve, others may want to even cut the cord with scissors if you prefer to leave things abruptly. For a slower process, watch the cord fall off of you. Perhaps it slowly dissolves. You may see the cord still attached to the people in the memory as they all fade from your mind's eye, or you may have to visit the memory a few times before you can actually cut the cord.

But, let the memory go, just as it is: a memory. Let the event depart, both physically and emotionally. Allow yourself to be free of this memory, as you are no longer burdened by it.

12. This exercise brings forth many emotions. It is completely normal to cry or sob. Just as we explored the pinwheel of emotions, this is a time when you may feel all the emotions simultaneously spinning within you. That is okay. Be gentle to yourself, and realize that you have released this memory or at least started the process to free yourself from this connection. You are starting the journey to being free, to living your life. Slowly return to the room, moving your body and opening your eyes Now just sit for a bit, and be kind to yourself.

Cutting the cord of connection was first presented to me after aiding in grief camps. Initially, I had a hard time getting my mind into the proper space, because I really was scared to recall the memories. Even the happy ones made me cry. (I wanted to go back to Disney World!) After practicing the exercise, along with "what's in the mirror of your mind's memory", I became very good at releasing memories that I felt hindered my daily life or held me back from success. When I let go of the word "plausibility", I cut the cord to the World Trade Center Towers, and I wrote my first word in this book.

Now we move into another activity, a behavioural task assignment that is called "The Forgiving Flowers". It's one of my favourites to assign to coaching clients. The activity is unique and very impactful. That being said, it is also the most resisted assignment. Clients will tell me, "Sure, I'll do it," and then week after week, when I ask how it went, they say, "Well, I really don't think it will work for me. I don't feel the need."

In my recovery, I've learned firsthand that we avoid what we think may hurt us, both physically and emotionally. As you recall, the bottle of burdens is where we keep our emotional pain, and when physical pain hits, we run to avoid it. We all have events or people that we can't change. Instead, we need to let go of them to move forward. We need to release our body and mind from the emotional connection that is pulling us backwards. We need to cut the cord of connections!

So give this activity a good try! If you're resistant, ask yourself why. What can it hurt to simply buy some flowers?

FORGIVING FLOWERS

This assignment is exactly as the name suggests. You're going to buy flowers.

1. Go out to a flower shop, grocery store, or garden. Choose flowers that represent the people in the memory that you just visualized. This could also be done with people that you presently want to let go of. These people might have died, or could presently be in your life; they could even be former friends that you had conflicts with, or an ex-partner. Choose anyone who is still actively in your thoughts or memories, or select a situation that you want to resolve or let go of.
2. Choose flowers that really remind you of these people, the memory or the event. (One woman needed to let go of her toxic family and specifically picked a flower for each relative. She was very specific about the colour, the smell, and the type.)
3. After you have picked your flowers, the next step is to take your bouquet home with you. Set your flowers up where you will see them daily. (Please note that from this day forth the flowers you choose for this activity may evoke memories in the future, so choose wisely.)
4. Now the hard part: sit down with a pen and paper,

and for each flower, write a small note about what this flower represents and how it feels to let that go. Write down how you are emotionally attached to this feeling, memory, or person, and perhaps include how this is physically affecting you. How is it holding you back from moving forward in life? Or maybe jot down how a behaviour has changed for you. You might currently fear something because of this event or person. (For instance, you might find it hard to date after a divorce.)
5. After writing a letter about each flower, and why you need to cut the cord of connection to these memories, events or people, place the paper next to the flowers.
6. Now walk away.

Let's check in here. The next day you will awake to these flowers. They may look beautiful and inviting. Or you might want to smell them. You might want to water them so that they live on. But think about it. Do you want to smell, nourish and help continue the growth of these flowers and what they represent?

These flowers are a reflection of your memory and your struggle with the fears of the memory, event or people. Just as we don't want to cultivate negative thoughts or memories that hold us back, we don't want to be drawn to the smell of these tainted flowers. So let's avoid helping the flowers grow. Instead you can talk to them, letting each one know how you feel, and how you no longer will engage in the memory or the feelings it triggers. Explain that, in time, you will no longer cry, sob, yell or feel the anger. You will let it all go. You will cut the cord, forgiving yourself for carrying this burden for so long. If you can, offer some forgiveness to the people connected to this memory.

As the days progress you will watch as your flowers die. You might also cry or feel sad, because you're letting go of something that truly impacted you and is a big part of you. But remember that you are only letting go of its *impact!* The memory is still yours, and the people may still be around, but they no longer impact your emotions, mind, body or ability to live a full life.

By now, you have watched your flowers fully die. It's probably taken a couple of weeks. You may have been surprised by how long it took. Was there a particular flower that survived the longest? Does that flower have a particular memory attached to it that was the hardest to let go of?

The next step, it is time to truly let your flowers go. Find a spot that brings you comfort and warms your heart. This could be a fishing spot or a stream, somewhere near a large body of water. Go to this place with your dead flowers. This might sound silly, but… Stand before the river, lake, body of water and look at your flowers. One by one, throw them into the water. With each one say goodbye to the memory, event, person or whatever it represented for you. Let it go! Watch as it floats away, is nipped by a fish, gets taken by a bird. Watch as it finds a new purpose. You are releasing the burden. These burdens that you fertilized to grow over your lifetime no longer live in the bottle inside of you. You are now clear from that memory or burden. Perhaps the bottle has a new purpose: to carry your light.

Presenting to large crowds makes any speaker wonder how he or she will be received. I once presented with my daughter to hundreds of young girls who came with their caregivers. Youth can be pretty critical, so I was more than a little nervous before this group. We spoke about self-esteem and our differences as young women. Being an older and hopefully a wiser woman, I wondered what I could say that would make them realize that their bottle could shine with light, not with their burdens.

Looking back, a friend had once said, "You're too happy for me." Another person had said, "You're just too much for me." These people never stopped being my friends, but I struggled with their words. I decided to cut the cords to friends who felt I was just "too much" for them. Once I completed the behavioural task assignments of cutting the cord and forgiving flowers, I was able to let go of negative people and their negative comments.

They noticed that my presence changed drastically; they questioned the change in my emotional connection to them. I explained that I felt the connection was not healthy. As they had mentioned they felt I was too happy or too much for them, in turn I explained it was affecting my confidence in who I truly was. I explained that it was for the best that we move in a positive direction that made us both feel fulfilled. They resisted, so I continued, saying that I just had to remove myself, emotionally, from the friendship.

Pondering all that just took place within my own adult friendships, as I stood arm-in-arm with my young daughter, I said, "When your light shines so bright that others are blinded, hand them a pair of sunglasses."

We should never dull our light just to fit in. We should be proud of our recoveries from trauma, our successes, our challenges, our failures, of everything we are, because it was all a learning process that brought us to this point. A point where our bottle does not carry our burdens, but rather carries our light!

CHAPTER TEN: WHY DO WE FEEL PAIN?

So far, we have looked at the many ways we handle pain, both emotionally and physically. We found that we sometimes think we can delete emotional pain from our minds by placing it in a bottle for safekeeping, which, in turn, only allows it to creep up on us and hurt us again and again. We may also give emotional pain an enormous amount of power. We may think that emotional pain will never heal, while physical pain, as we have witnessed, can heal at times. But also we realize that emotional pain can affect and does affect our physical being. Pain is something we want to avoid in life. Who purposely wants to explore why we feel emotional pain? Well, I DO!

I have witnessed so much emotional pain in my life, that I became truly interested in why we avoid emotional pain, rather than seek realizations and changes for the better. Think: when you're in physical pain your body is telling you something is wrong. You seek medical help for the pain and perhaps even remove the issue.

What about the emotional pain we feel—does it have a purpose? Many great gurus, for a lack of a better word, suggest that pain has a bigger purpose than we as humans want to accept or realize. It is truly hard to look emotional pain in the eye and ask, "Why?" To some, it even might be an insult to ask the why question.

I've often wondered why my brother died young, or why I had a cancer scare. Why do we all experience so much emotional pain only to store it in a bottle of burdens? I learned first-hand what happens when someone allows the bottle of burdens to stay sealed. Even after the doctor spoke to me regarding a dangerous infection in my leg ("If you don't talk about it, it will physically show up in your body."), I was still in denial.

So many of us live in denial. We "can't see straight" (for a lack of better words). Our perception has been tainted so very much that the lens we look through is foggy. Our shell is strong, and our masks are on! We may become numb physically. Pain is no longer an issue, because we don't feel anymore. At times our eyes look glossy, as if we hear, but have no real comprehension of what is being said. We're going through the motions of life but not really living it. To find our bodies again, we must be willing to feel (emotionally, physically and mentally).

I worked with a colleague who was numb with fear. We attended a few conferences together, and every time we parked the car, he would scan the parking lot. One day, I said, "What are you looking for?"

"He replied in true police fashion, "You never know what can happen."

I chuckled, replying, "Do you ever let your guard down?"

He replied quickly, "Nope."

Once we were preparing to do a workshop together, in which the participants connected to their bodies by walking on the grass or rocks. (He, of course, wanted to walk on fire.) I explained that this would allow the participants to feel again, to let their guards down. He thought it sounded "dumb". I said, "Let's try it."

He quickly removed his shoes in the parking lot (yup.... to prove a point). He started to walk, and I saw his face change. He said, "Wow, I have sensitive feet."

I said, "Tell me, do you only feel it in your feet?"

He replied, "You are strange, Red, but I feel scared, like I can't run if something bad happens."

Truly, nothing bad was going to happen in a parking lot up north in the middle of nowhere. But as he continued walking, he was very intrigued by the fear he felt when his guard was down. I removed my shoes and joined him. As my bare feet hit the cement, I felt the contact resonate up my body as if to say, "I am alive!!!!"

Are you alive? I challenge you to remove your own shoes and start walking on the grass. Think of a baby, who will usually pull its feet up from the tickle of the grass. Then, feel the cold, the thin pieces, the wetness or maybe dry grass. Let your eyes close and feel with your feet. You may be surprised how grounded and connected you feel to the earth. My colleague truly embraced this activity. He challenges me every year, as he steps into the snow, in the dead cold of winter, in his bare feet and sends me a picture requesting one back.

Muay Thai boxing appealed to me because it, too,

is practiced in bare feet. When you feel emotionally numb, bare-footed martial arts could be appealing. The first few months were a struggle as I tried to learn the moves. Overthinking made it much harder, so I would step back from the bag and let my mind release my body. Then I would open my eyes and let my body's natural rhythm take me where it should be. It felt amazing hitting the bag, learning combinations, kicking in various ways.

Then one day my coach—a large, square statue of a man—said, "Red, why don't you take it to the ring?"

I heard a few people say, "She won't."

I nervously replied, "Okay," as if it was no problem.

I stepped into the ring to look up at a throat of tattoos. He started saying all sorts of Muay Thai combinations, and to my surprise, I kept up. Yet I was becoming exhausted and he heard me panting. I started to exhale with a moan.

He said, "Yes, that is your warrior call. Do it! It is a way to get air and release power."

Suddenly I pulled my sparring partner off balance and started to knee him with all my might. I felt this energy come over me. I saw images of my career. People in my arms crying. Feeling enraged from all the disasters of the world. I even flashed back to a street scene that unfolded after 9/11, to an imposing group of men… Then I heard the coach say, "Hey, keep it in the ring."

To my coach and sparring partner that had been just a good fight, but to me, it was the recollection of a memory that had haunted me without my realizing it. My newfound expression of feeling my senses through boxing goes without saying: the core purpose of the fight was to challenge my physical body and in turn, yet again, it had connected with my emotions, my being, and they were working together. I share this rather disturbing boxing match with you so you see how the body does encompass our memories and trauma. I had no idea my mind would flow to a time in my life that I felt threatened and then evoke my body to go into warrior mode. You have to be prepared when you step back into your physical body and challenge it, it carries much more than you think.

My favourite practice to feel and connect with my body is simply nature. I will walk for hours within the woods, hearing, smelling, watching and feeling my surroundings. Most tragedies I aided in were like walking into sheer chaos. I would spend my days and nights working in trauma. Hearing the question, "Why does the (emotional) pain hurt so much? Why… why …why?"

I, too, pondered the same questions for years. I would often go on mini sabbaticals or walks in various areas where I was deployed or aiding in the hopes to find the calm of nature, often leading me on the best adventures ever! While aiding in the mountains of Alberta, I once wandered off into the woods with my snow shoes on, as well as my winter pants and my new red down jacket that could stand the cold of Canada. During my walks I openly talk to myself, checking in with myself to see how I am.

Try it. Ask yourself, "How are you today? How are you feeling?"

My self-talk would often be about events or experiences that I was presently involved with or challenged with. During this walk my skin could feel the cold of the

Alberta wind blowing. As I trooped through the snow, looking over a beautiful mountain down to a valley filled with snow-sprinkled rocks, I heard footsteps. I turned quickly to see a moose. At first glance I was shocked, and then out of the trees came a baby moose.

I quickly pulled my cell phone out and took a picture. As I pulled the phone down, I saw that the mother moose had locked eyes with me. I could feel her fear of me rise. I started to slowly move backwards, which didn't work well in snow shoes. I saw her slowly look back at her "foe".

All of a sudden I was pulled from my gaze with mama moose, as I heard a voice say, "Don't go near her. She will charge you." I turned to see a man with all the same gear as me... but he was accompanied by three beautiful Husky dogs. His dark, long, black hair covered his face.

As he explained, "Moose, when threatened, are not the kindest of animals." He swept his hair behind his ears revealing a dark complexion and brown eyes, and he quickly said, "You're not from around here."

I replied, "No."

He continued. "I know who you are."

I laughed, and said, "Who?"

He replied, "You're the lady on the street signs."

I laughed again. "Yeah, a little large for my liking."

He then said, "I heard you speak the other night."

I was taken aback, thinking, *Wow, I came out here to get away.*

Interrupting my thoughts, he said, "ᑲ ᓲᐦᑫᔨᒧᕽ sohkeyimohk," (in Cree).

"Pardon?" I replied.

He repeated himself, "Courage. You have great courage. Clearly takes a lot of courage to take on a mother moose." He then went on to tell me that my courage and strength to help others was a gift. He believed that messengers came in many forms, including wolves, foxes and six-foot redheads. He assured me my message was being heard by his community in a time of need.

As we walked with his three huskies, he shared his memories of the land under our feet. He carried many stories that he wanted to share, stories about his culture and how his land healed him. As I reached my destination he placed a feather in my hand. "The light and the dark shadows foxed him." I looked at him, bewildered. He said, "Don't allow your memories to fool you that there is only darkness. Allow the light to give you the courage to share your gift."

As I continued to walk I saw the face of the mother moose in my mind's eye, how she was willing to fight, to give her life for her child. My self-talk during my sabbatical that day was surrounding the "why" question. The man saw my ability to share my grief as courageous. Was that not a reflection that I saw? My goal was to help others in their pain to realize they are not alone. My self-talk continued: "Why do you keep going towards pain?" Then I answered myself: "Because the pain I feel is from the depth of my love for others."

The simplicity of the reason why we feel so much emotional pain flowed into my thoughts and being. We feel pain and grieve so very much because we love so deeply. We love with all our hearts, and we allow our being to fully love another person whom we lost. When we allow ourselves to love, without barriers or conditions, we are fully living. But when that love is challenged by grief in all its forms, we feel enormous pain. That pain is so very strong that we bottle it. We make our shells strong like steel and put on our masks.

The courage the man saw was the courage to LOVE again, fully. You love someone or something unconditionally with all your heart. The pain is a result of the courage to LOVE fully. That is a gift in itself. The question is not, "Why?" It is, "Do you have the courage to love and live fully again?"

CHAPTER ELEVEN: CONTINUING TO LIVE

"It is not what happens to you in life that creates who you are, it is how you handle it that truly creates who you are." This realization comes after you have mastered your ability to guide your own destiny, acknowledge that bad things will happen, death will still impact you, and trauma of all kinds will still be there.

I traveled far up north to a hospice where I was placed in the nicest bed and breakfast. The community was ecstatic to welcome me as their speaker on death and dying, and had plastered my face around the whole town. (Seeing my face on billboards on a highway was hard to swallow.) The home I stayed in was owned by two men who had created a beautiful life together. The décor dated back to the 70's, and outside my quaint bedroom was an old high-fidelity record player with numerous records leaning up against it. Each morning one of the men would play one of the many records and let old jazz music fill the house. Adorning the windows of the house were tapestries of all colours, while glass-beaded curtains separated the rooms. The place was truly an adventure for the eyes, and the hosts were absolutely exceptional. On the day of my presentation, a vintage car drove up to take me to the community centre. I felt like I was stepping back in time.

Entering the building, I smiled, greeted and graciously hugged so many people. It truly felt amazing to be seen as someone special in this small community. As I took the podium, the faces in the audience stared back at me as if to say, "Please help us." I started to share my stories, my lessons, my teachings, my beliefs on grief. My eyes wandered to the window as I heard a cow mooing. I giggled to myself, thinking that all was there, as it should be, animals, people, sorrow and, most of all, hope. The evening was one of great love, acceptance, heavy conversation and good food.

The next morning I was invited for breakfast by a few of the organizers. (This time, my skin stuck against the leather seat of that vintage car.) We soon arrived at a lovely greasy spoon restaurant, and I was so excited about having eggs and bacon! I let my guard down and took off the professional speaker mask. I was just me, the same me at home with my friends and family. As I spoke, an older lady's face started to change, her eyes became sadder. I stopped mid-sentence and said, "Are you okay?"

She leaned closer to me and looked directly into my eyes and said, "Wow, you're just normal, like there is nothing special about you? I am so disappointed." Yet she was not being mean. Her belief was that in order to achieve what I had, I needed to be special.

I then touched her hand and said, " What you have realized is not what you think. You have just realized that you don't have to be special to achieve greatness. That you to have the ability to change the world in any way you choose. Essentially, you have realized you too can achieve this, and that you haven't tried nor thought you could. Your disappointment is within yourself, not me."

She was completely taken aback. In my mind, I had complimented her. Yet on the flip side, I had said that she was not using her greatness. She immediately excused herself, and I knew that I had hit a core belief.

As the breakfast came to an end the lady appeared again. She then shared that she had dreams of being an author. I replied, "The only thing that makes me special is that I look fear in the eye. What we fear is what we don't know. So get knowing.... learn about what you fear. I feared death. Upon facing my fear of death, the realization that it has a purpose, a place and a gift to give us all, was my freeing moment. I realized that I feared many things. Every time I encounter fear I look at it straight in the eye and say, 'Teach me'.

We all have a story inside of us, of adventure, sadness, grief, happiness and so on. The individual's perception affects how they present it to the world. That being said, moving forward and putting what you have learned into practice is by far the hardest part. Think of people who endlessly educate themselves, but never make the move towards a career. Think of the person who stays at the same job, and then complains about it daily. Think of the person who knows everything about losing weight but never puts it into practice. Why? Perhaps fear.

Fear can come in many forms and is an extremely strong emotional response. It arises when someone feels threatened or feels they will encounter a dangerous situation that will cause pain. The body clicks into action, and either you fight or spring into flight. In our caveman years this was a key component to survival. In today's world, we are usually prepared for the danger to come (whether storms or wars). But after unpredictable events, our fear radar is reactivated to the level of a phobia. Then the phobia can transform and take the form of a belief.

Young children affected by terrorist attacks on New York had formed an interesting belief that the children of other countries had formed also. During my time in the schools, I noticed a student playing with blocks. When I approached the student asking what she was creating, she replied, "The Trade Towers." She continued by placing a red block on top of each tower while saying, "This is a red flashing light on top so the planes don't hit it again." She explained to me that this would solve the issue of the plane not seeing the tower correctly.

When I was back in Canada, I was invited into various schools to answer questions, calm fears and share some ways to understand our emotions surrounding all the media coverage of 9/11. Again, out of the corner of my eye, I saw a young boy who was creating a tower. I wandered towards him asking, "What are you creating?" With a strong, confident voice he said, "The Trade Towers, but mine are safe."

I cocked my head and said, "Why are yours safe?"

He said, "This red block is a siren so the planes hear that the tower is in front of them." His words had echoed the girl in New York.

In their minds, planes were at fault for the towers going

down. These two students had never flown, and so many people would wonder why they were scared of planes. They had created a phobia, an irrational belief, from the fear they had experienced, created it all on their own! This is a perfect example of how even young minds can create phobias, burdens, memories that tend to follow them into adulthood.

As a teenager, I knew that if I loved someone, there was a chance that they might die. The phobia of loving someone, mixed with the belief that loving is losing, became an irrational belief. My husband, then my boyfriend, was able to identify this at a very young age, and he would play the song "Desperado": "You better let somebody love you, before it's too late." I would look into his eyes thinking, *Do I take the chance? What if he dies too?* If I hadn't challenged my irrational belief that loving results in losing, I might have gone numb and even lost my physical being in the midst of it all.

Feeling emotions—your body, all of it—is good for you! As we've seen, we can continuously modify our memories and beliefs for continuous growth, however, most irrational beliefs are created from fear. We also create excuses that are endorsed by our irrational beliefs and derived by fear. What we learned through the chapters is that we have control over our minds and bodies. We can alter our thoughts gradually. We can face the fear within our bottle of burdens and challenge the memories, which resonate within our bodies, to be positive.

What comes next is to challenge yourself! Challenge your relationships, challenge your beliefs, challenge your physical abilities, challenge your whole world!

In order to continue to live we must be willing to grow in all areas of our lives. Have you ever wanted to write a book? Fly a plane? Own a business? Be more positive? Lose some weight? Let's set our goals!

First, take a step back and jot down three things you would like to try or achieve. (Kinda like a bucket list, but no one is dying at the end!) Title them goals one, two and three.

Next, go back to your bottle of burdens. Now, hopefully, it is somewhat empty, leaving space for your light to shine. Look at each goal and ask yourself what is holding you back. Is it a burden, memory or a past trauma? Write down next to each goal what is holding you back from achieving it.

Finally, using the tools from this book, rid or clear yourself from the emotional and physical effects of this burden in your daily life. Take a moment now to look over the previous chapters, and then select the tool that looks right for the task.

This practice of goal setting and exploring from a different perspective can help not only with achieving goals, but with building the blocks of confidence to try new things and to explore all that life has to offer.

CHAPTER TWELVE:
THE PERSPECTIVE THAT
MATTERS IS YOUR OWN!

Often when a parent dies, adult children start living differently. Many have said to me, with great guilt, "I feel free." They are baffled by this feeling. Some will leave long term marriages they stayed in for the sake of their parents. Some will embrace their sexual preference. Some will go on long-dreamed-of adventures. Why?

It is believed that our parents are our first relationships, and the most impacting, so it is only natural for children to want a parent to be proud of them. At times parents are proud and the child can't even see it or vice versa. So when this relationship is over, the adult child realizes that life is short and that the legacy of their parents lives with them. They begin to question how they want to live the rest of their lives now that the anchor to their ship has lifted, leaving the boat free to sail.

Many coaching clients at this stage do amazing things. One packed up and travelled across Canada with the whole family in tow; another started up a franchise with great success; and another flew a plane without ever having set foot in one until then. If your mindset was that today might be your last day on earth, how would you be thinking?

People ask, "How can you always be smiling and so happy considering what you do for a living?"

I always reply, "I am reminded daily that I am lucky to be alive."

It is hard to explain what I do. I can say that I am an author or a humanitarian, or a professional speaker. But really what I do is this: take out five bucks and look at it. Now crumple it up, throw it on the ground and step on it. (You'd better be doing this!) Now pick up the five dollars and try to rip it apart. Now, no matter what you do to the five dollars, you can tape it back together; it is always worth five bucks. You can still buy yourself that coffee at Tim Hortons.

This is essentially what I do. I teach people that no matter what happens in life, if a person has been stepped on, bullied, divorced, experienced the death of a loved one, no matter what we have experienced in life, we are as valuable as the day we were born. We as humans don't lose value as we age, and just like money, we always have value! We remain as valuable as the day we were born!

One thing is for sure: people change over time. It is inevitable. We evolve. The person may alter his or her beliefs after an encounter makes them see things much differently.

Let me share a funny story about belief modification at its best. Often after being deployed or aiding, I would meet up with some friends at a pub in Niagara Falls. But this time I went alone, basking in my own company. I sat there and had a few drinks and talked away with hometown locals. It was nice to eat a good burger and just chat. The bartender was this young girl with amazing dark brown hair. She wore tight jeans and a low-cut Coors Light t-shirt, and she rocked it all.

As she dragged an old washcloth across the bar, she said, "What brings you in here every couple of months?"

I cracked a half smile and replied, "Work."

I saw the brown of the wood become more vibrant as she continued to wash the bar. She asked, "What line of work is that?"

I replied, "Humanitarian in the field of grief."

She suddenly stopped washing the bar and looked directly at me, "What exactly do you do?"

I rattled off, "Well this wasn't a chosen career when I was fourteen my brother fell over the Niagara Falls gorge then I wrote a book called, *Where Is Robert?* and over 6,000 were used at Ground Zero"

But before I could continue, she gasped, exclaiming, "What!?"

I said, "Yeah the best part is I then was asked to aid in other world tragedies…"

She gasped again, then said, "You're drunk! That's a good story, crazy lady."

The next minute I heard her on the phone calling me a cab. I left that night shrugging my shoulders, thinking no one believed me.

A few months passed, and I thought nothing more about the encounter with the bartender. For many people, it is hard to accept that we, as humans, need another human to help us through times of grief. No one wants to see the big, scary monster ("plausibility") or accept it can even exist. Also, if I was that great or did these amazing things, why would I be sitting at a bar, alone?

But I found myself in the same spot months later, once again heading to the same bar for my routine downtime. I sat on the same stool, where the wood of the bar is just a little more golden. To my surprise the same bartender came swinging through the back door. She saw me and immediately connected. I noticed her hair was shorter and that her look was intense.

She approached me hesitantly, and I could feel that something was not quite right. She reached out to put her hand on mine and said, "I have been waiting for you to come in again." She then shared, "I pack fish in newspapers in the back when customers order them to go. After you left that night, I was in the back a few days later rolling some fish up, and when I looked down, I saw your picture in the paper. I was so shocked as I read all about you. OMG, you were not lying that night. I am such an ass. I am so sorry. I felt utterly awful for the way I reacted to you."

I stopped her mid-sentence and said it was okay, and that it was perhaps a lot to hear. She then proceeded to buy me dinner as we chatted all night.

The bartender could not believe that I could be an average person, sitting eating a burger with a beer. She had an irrational belief that successful people don't go to a bar, act kind, or chat with others. Her irrational belief was changed that night simply when I walked back into the bar, showing her that we are equals.

People's disbelief also shows up on Facebook. I posted something on the September 11th anniversary, a big hug to all the children I was with at Ground Zero. Someone actually commented on the post saying, "Is this a joke? No, you weren't."

Again, I've come to realize that people have beliefs about others, believing that if you're successful, you don't frequent bars, or share on FB. (It is funny to hear them talk about your book or you as an author. I even recall someone actually trying to sell me my own book at a grief conference!) People project themselves and their beliefs onto others. It is their core beliefs, experiences, and traumas that are creating the lens through which they perceive us.

It is not what we experience in life, it is how we choose to handle it, how we choose to learn from lived experience in order to live a fuller life.

CHAPTER THIRTEEN: HOW FITTING

Life has taught me so many lessons. I have shattered many bottles of burdens, cracked many egg shells, made many masks and worn a few as well, along with so much more. I have experienced so much grief, so much death and so much pain. It has taken me on a journey of education and emotional and physical exploration. This has all left me pondering. What's next? What am I dying to do now?

Well, I am dying to live fully. I am dying to live without fear. I am dying to cut the cord of connection to memories, people, and events that don't support a healthy life. To show the real me, not the mask others see me in. I am dying to feel my emotions and all their varied colours. To live connected to nature and our universe.

But as I come to this realization, I also question, "Is living fully obtainable after so much trauma and brokenness within me?" Seeing death isn't something you get over. It is integrated into who we are. Death can occur at every stage of life and is not something we can fix or medicate or change.

My lesson: the key to happiness is balance, balance that is integrated into our lives and practiced daily. Just as I was able to balance imbalanced breasts, I was able to learn how to balance my career. I was able to learn how to balance my emotions and how to recognize when the balance is off in all areas of my life. We simply complete this process and move forward. Goals are set to keep the balance, self-care is practiced to keep the balance, self-reflection is needed to keep balance, self-education and exploration is essential for balance and lastly gratitude for the balance and all that we have.

On the tenth anniversary of 9/11, I was interviewed by the media and asked to share how my life had changed since aiding. I listened as the reporter recalled the events of that day. It was surreal, like I was watching a movie, one that truly impacted me. My eyes welled at each image that reminded me of the families I spent time with, the children I worked with. As the reporter prepared me for the interview, the photographer flashed lights to make sure it all looked good, and the makeup artist touched up the shine. As the click of the recorder went on, I could feel my heart start to quicken. I started to realize how much had changed in my life.

About ten months before, while in New York City with my family, I had some huge realizations. First, why did I travel to New York City so close to the ten-year anniversary? I recall being very emotional on the trip, and I knew I was having trouble with my emotions, and that my family had no idea why, nor did I. I recall standing on a street corner in Little Italy and starting to cry, while my husband watched, not knowing what to do with me. My kids, fourteen and sixteen, were rather confused by my emotional outburst. I blamed it on all the walking and attempted to calm myself. At this point I was not practicing balancing in my own life at all.

While dining at a famous Italian bistro, I blurted out, "What if we have another child?"

Immediately I saw my husband's face look confused. My eldest son exclaimed, "Are you crazy? You have gone nuts!"

I looked at my daughter, and she said, "How will this affect my life, mainly financially?"

I explained that I didn't know what was to come next in my life, and that I felt my career took me away from experiencing their childhood fully.

My husband said, "Are you sure?"

To my surprise he was open to the idea, but made it clear that there was to be only one more child. After lunch, I secretly picked up a baby magazine. I flipped through the pages, thinking that this really could become a reality. *Could I actually have another baby?* I started to feel my body react to my emotions... I was excited.

When we returned home we decided to let things be and see what happened. The kids and my hubby were in major disbelief, as I was thirty-nine. I, too, was doubting that it was even possible. The very next month I was pregnant. As a family, we all piled into the car to go to our first ultrasound. I laughed as they said my name in the waiting room and we all stood up. I lay there in awe as we all stared at the machine.

The nurse asked my family to guess the baby's sex, and they moved in closer, looking harder. The nurse said, "You're correct", pointing to my daughter, "it is a girl." (I saw the disappointment in the men's faces.)

As the months progressed I got bigger and bigger. We had decided to work with midwives and have a home birth (another area of great debate with lots of differences and perspectives). We spent endless hours discussing the perfect name as we proceeded to buy all the best stuff for our new arrival.

Finally, one day, I woke up knowing she was coming. The midwives showed up and, to my surprise, my older children wanted to be a part of the birth. My husband called my family, and they rushed over. I recall the DIY channel was playing on the TV as I sat giving birth in the living room. It was a fairly quick labour. I won't lie. (When midwives say, "No drugs," they *mean* no drugs, so seriously consider this when doing a home birth. It hurts like no other pain.) I had let my mind go and allowed my body to do what it was built to do. I had to trust my body. I searched for balance and shortly felt this sense of calm.

My eyes scanned my family as they all stood with me in this pain. It was so much like death: we grieve together, we heal together. Death strips us naked and is the only thing that equalizes mankind. But, here was something else that was having the same impact: birth. We put all our differences aside to welcome life to our family.

All of a sudden I was jolted out of my realization by a cry. I looked down as a baby girl was placed on my tummy. Everyone was crying, embracing, laughing and counting toes. She was perfect in every way, and she was big! Together, we were placed in our family bed.

This time I wanted to really do things the way

nature intended, to the best of my ability. As the days followed, our nameless little girl made us all smile, laugh and cry, as my older children learned about cloth diapers. I was so excited that my imbalanced breast fed wonderfully. I realized that, when in New York, I had been experiencing PTSD and didn't know it. I was reminded of the death I had experienced that brought me to my knees, and I knew that I was still bottling my pain, as I had when my brother died. But now I could see that death and life go together, hand and hand.

An Indigenous Elder once told me, "Cleanse the death from you. Do not bring death home." Now I have brought life home. I asked myself, "Is living fully obtainable after so much trauma and brokenness within me?" I have learned that the trauma and the brokenness have not devalued me; rather, they have increased my value. My exchange rate is high, and I am worth so much more than I will ever realize.

So many of us are worth more than we can see. When others share their stories with me, they often start with, "It is nothing great." To learn their stories is amazing, and not only does it help me see a different person's experiences and perspectives, but it helps others. We need to share our stories for the education of generations to come as we all learn through each other. Through my life and my experiences I have come to learn this:

Death sees no difference. Death does not see colour, faith, religion, wealth or fame; it is the only equalizer of discrimination. Death does not care who you are, or what you are. It cares to teach you that together we stand, together we grieve, together we heal

And I now also believe this:

> Living sees no difference. Living does not see colour, faith, religion, wealth or fame; it is the only equalizer of discrimination. Living does not care who you are, or what you are. It cares to teach you that together we stand, together we live, together we heal.

When we live fully we don't see differences; we don't judge others based on wealth, colour, faith or discriminate. We live to the fullest, and we are so busy living, laughing and loving that we don't have time to compare. Not only do we recognize ourselves for what we are capable of, but we are open to loving and encouraging other people. In death, we unite; in the creation of life, we unite. Is it possible to live fully? The answer is a simple, "YES!" For, as I write these words, I am living the life I was dying to live.

(Seriously, did I just end the book on chapter number 13?)

ABOUT THE AUTHOR

Christine Dernederlanden C.B.T., C.T.S.S. resides with her family in the Niagara Region of Ontario, Canada. She is a wife, mother, sister, aunt, friend, entrepreneur, author, professional speaker, coach and tea addict. Her great passion is helping children, adults and families cope with grief and trauma.

Christine is certified by the Association of Traumatic Stress Specialists as a Certified Trauma Services Specialist and is a member of the American Academy of Experts in Traumatic Stress, with a certification in Bereavement Trauma. Her academic affiliations include Niagara University, Oklahoma Traumatology, Brock University, the University of Wisconsin and National Centre for P.T.S.D. As a member of the Toronto International Coaching Federation, Christine also offers professional coaching, writing and speaking for clients including corporations, small businesses, individuals, government agencies, and non-profits.

A personal loss early in life led Christine to write her very first book, entitled, Where is Robert? This grief kit aided more than 6,000 families affected by the 9/11 terrorist attacks and earned Christine a certificate of appreciation from former U.S. Secretary of Defense Donald. H Rumsfeld. Her second publication, H.U.G.S.: Helping Children Understand Grief Sessions, was inspired by work at the grief camps that she co-facilitated with the Friendship Ambassadors (a group which fosters dialogues with the United Nations and Lions International). For the subsequent article "Putting All My Problems In Perspective", Christine was awarded the 2001 Standard Literary Prize.

Christine has been recognized internationally for her work as a humanitarian. In 2000, she founded Robert's Press, Canada's Grief Resource Centre. As a result, she was named one of Niagara's most successful businesswomen, as well as a 2001 finalist for Woman of The Year and Entrepreneur of The Year. In 2002, Christine was awarded the Leadership and Communication Award by the Toastmasters Public Speaking Organization for her exceptional communication and professional speaking skills.

Seeing a need for the exploration of empathy and courage, she later created the Empathy Bear, "an everlasting plush friend", which is used worldwide to bring comfort and compassion to the grieving. Her claymation story titled Where is My Courage? supported the families of the 2016 Fort McMurray, Alberta wildfires. In 2017, she earned the Distinguished Alumni of the Year Award and was also selected as finalist for the 2019 Community Impact Award.

Two decades working in the field of grief and trauma inspired the author to write Thank You: The Power of Presence with the Grieving and Dying. In 2020, responding to losses due to Covid-19, Christine released Cora and the Corona. More than 7,500 copies of the book were donated to mental health essential services, and a follow up program was created to foster children's mental well-being during the pandemic. Today, with her most recent book, Christine continues to inspire others through her personal reflections.

Reach out to the author at www.christinedernederlanden.ca

www.ingramcontent.com/pod-product-compliance
Lightning Source LLC
Chambersburg PA
CBHW072055290426
44110CB00014B/1686